D1094730

To Mexico with Taylor and Scott
1845–1847

Primary Sources in
American History

CONSULTING EDITOR
Grady McWhiney, University of British Columbia

To Mexico with Taylor and Scott 1845-1847

EDITED BY GRADY McWHINEY

University of British Columbia

SUE McWHINEY

BLAISDELL PUBLISHING COMPANY

A Division of Ginn and Company

WALTHAM, MASSACHUSETTS / TORONTO / LONDON

to C. S. S. and M. H. M.

Foreword

Thorough understanding of the events and trends that make up our history cannot be acquired merely by reading textbook interpretations. It is essential also to study the basis of such interpretations. *The Primary Sources in American History Series* provides the student with materials in the form of letters, diaries, memoirs, pamphlets, and newspaper accounts written during or shortly after major historical events — documents up to now buried in the library and often unavailable.

Edited and introduced by a leading scholar, each volume either concentrates on discussion of a given topic in contemporary letters, newspaper articles, and essays or presents new editions of classic eyewitness accounts of significant events. Though generations removed from an actual occurrence, the student has the opportunity to understand it in depth and to apply his analytical and critical powers to it. He then also can compare his own interpretations with those provided by general histories, biographies, and monographs.

GRADY MCWHINEY

Contents

Introduction

The war between the United States and Mexico which occurred more than a century ago can still excite debate. In 1962 Robert F. Kennedy replied to Indonesian students who asked about the American invasion of Mexico in 1846: "I think we were unjustified. I do not think we can be proud of that episode." But a United States senator and a governor objected; they insisted that the causes for which Americans fought Mexicans were just. Such disagreement was merely the continuation of opposing positions taken in 1847. At that time a Whig editor denounced the war as "unnecessary" — "a spectacle of backsliding and crime over which angels may weep." He charged that the United States was "engaged in war with a sister republic . . . for the real purpose . . . of effecting a forcible dismemberment of that republic, and of profiting . . . by the spoils." Though many people supported this view, it was challenged by Democratic Senator Lewis Cass, who probably spoke for a majority of the American people when he stated that Mexican injustice had caused the war. "Before peace is established," announced Cass, "we have a right to require a reasonable indemnity, either pecuniary or territorial, or both, for . . . injuries we have sustained. Such a compensation is just in itself and in strict accordance with the usages of nations."

Whether justified or not — and that is a moral rather than a historical question — the Mexican War significantly shaped American history and deserves more attention than it usually receives in textbooks and lectures. "To dismiss the war with Mexico as nothing more than a parade through the chaparral," cautions a scholar, "is to lose sight of its broader significance." The Treaty of Guadalupe Hidalgo, which ended the conflict, gave the United States possession of more than a half-million square miles of Mexican territory. This acquisition of new land made possible the California Gold Rush of 1849; it made necessary the Compromise of 1850; it reopened the question of slavery in the territories, which only the Civil War settled; and it left an awkward legacy which hampered American relations with Latin American and other countries.

The war's influence upon American military thought and practice, though often ignored, was also profound. Outnumbered by Mexican soldiers in every battle, United States forces successfully invaded northern Mexico, seized New Mexico and California, and swept inland from Vera Cruz to occupy Mexico City. Two years of uninterrupted victories gave many Americans an exaggerated appreciation of their martial ability. Courage, some people believed, accounted for the American triumph; others insisted that superior technology, tactics, and training defeated the Mexicans. General Scott claimed that if he had been without the services of the young officers who had learned the techniques of war at the United States Military Academy "the war . . . probably would have lasted some four or five years, with, in its first half, more defeats than victories." Many of these West Point graduates would have the opportunity to display their military skill again in the 1860s. Most of the principal Union and Confederate generals learned the tactics and strategy they would practice in the Civil War while campaigning in Mexico with Taylor and Scott.

It is impossible to understand the Mexican War, or any war, without knowledge of the military campaigns and the men who fought them. Too many instructors mistakenly conclude that

neither they nor their students need to know what happened
in a war; they frequently skip from the causes of a war to its
aftermath. This is both illogical and unscholarly because war
itself is part of a sequence which includes events leading up to
the actual conflict and those which result from it. To understand a war's outcome, one must study how that war was
waged — its strategy, tactics, logistics, and technology — as
well as the reactions of those who participated in it.

The military events of the Mexican War have been described
in numerous books, but until now no collection of eyewitness
accounts by participants in that war was readily available. Because primary source material on Manifest Destiny, the causes
of the Mexican War, and the diplomatic and political events of
the late 1840s has already appeared in paperback volumes, none
of these topics is emphasized in this work. It is devoted entirely
to the observations of men who fought under the American
banner in Mexico. These soldiers, a mixed lot, included regular
army enlistees, often foreigners; civilian volunteers from different sections of the country; old soldiers, veterans of the War
of 1812 and Indian skirmishes; and young West Pointers.

Some of the men who accompanied Taylor and Scott left
vivid accounts of their experiences in Mexico. From various
primary sources — letters, diaries, reports, and memoirs — we
have selected material which describe and analyze the major
campaigns and reveal, in the words of those who were there,
the reactions of diverse men to places and people and war. It
should be noted that the views expressed in the following documents are merely those of articulate individuals, not necessarily
the opinions of others of similar rank or background.

GRADY   MC WHINEY

SUE   MC WHINEY

PART ONE
*With Taylor from Corpus Christi
to Buena Vista*

CHAPTER 1 The Army
Assembled

After the United States annexed Texas, relations with Mexico
quickly deteriorated and war seemed likely. Especially disputed was ownership of southern Texas, between the Nueces
River and the Rio Grande. To support the American claim
President James K. Polk sent several thousand soldiers under
General Zachary Taylor to Corpus Christi in May 1845;
through the summer and fall more troops arrived at Taylor's
camp.

Among the reinforcements was a twenty-three-year-old second lieutenant of the Fourth Infantry, Ulysses Simpson Grant
(1822–1885), destined to become the Civil War's most celebrated Union general. Though a graduate of the United
States Military Academy in 1843, Grant had no intention of
becoming a professional soldier. The confrontation with Mexico troubled him. He regarded the annexation of Texas as an
aggressive act, and he believed President Polk planned to provoke war. Later Grant wrote: "I had a horror of the Mexican
War . . . only I had not moral courage enough to resign. . . .
I considered my supreme duty was to my flag." In his memoirs,
written just before his death, he recalled the military preparations at Corpus Christi.

ULYSSES S. GRANT
Personal Memoirs of U. S. Grant, *2 vols.*
New York, Charles L. Webster & Co., 1885, Vol. I, pp. 61–67

Early in September the regiment left New Orleans for Corpus Christi, now in Texas. Ocean steamers were not then common, and the passage was made in sailing vessels. At that time there was not more than three feet of water in the channel at the outlet of Corpus Christi Bay; the debarkation, therefore, had to take place by small steamers, and at an island in the channel called Shell Island, the ships anchoring some miles out from shore. This made the work slow, and as the army was only supplied with one or two steamers, it took a number of days to effect the landing of a single regiment with its stores, camp and garrison equipage, etc. There happened to be pleasant weather while this was going on, but the land-swell was so great that when the ship and steamer were on opposite sides of the same wave they would be at considerable distance apart. The men and baggage were let down to a point higher than the lower deck of the steamer, and when ship and steamer got into the trough between the waves, and were close together, the load would be drawn over the steamer and rapidly run down until it rested on the deck.

After I had gone ashore, and had been on guard several days at Shell Island, quite six miles from the ship, I had occasion for some reason or other to return on board. While on the *Suviah* — I think that was the name of our vessel — I heard a tremendous racket at the other end of the ship, and much and excited sailor language, such as "damn your eyes," etc. In a moment or two the captain, who was an excitable little man, dying with consumption, and not weighing much over a hundred pounds, came running out, carrying a sabre nearly as large and as heavy as he was, and crying that his men had mutinied. It was necessary to sustain the captain without question, and in a few minutes all the sailors charged with mutiny were in irons. I rather felt for a time a wish that I had not gone aboard just then. As the men charged with mutiny submitted to being placed in irons without resistance, I always doubted if they knew that they had mutinied until they were told.

By the time I was ready to leave the ship again I thought I had learned enough of the working of the double and single pulley, by which passengers were let down from the upper deck of the ship to the steamer below, and determined to let myself down without assistance. Without saying anything of my intentions to any one, I mounted the railing, and taking hold of the centre rope, just below the upper block, I put one foot on the hook below the lower block, and stepped off. Just as I did so some one called out "hold on." It was too late. I tried to "hold on" with all my might, but my heels went up, and my head went down so rapidly that my hold broke, and I plunged head foremost into the water, some twenty-five feet below, with such velocity that it seemed to me I never would stop. When I came to the surface again, being a fair swimmer, and not having lost my presence of mind, I swam around until a bucket was let down for me, and I was drawn up without a scratch or injury. I do not believe there was a man on board who sympathized with me in the least when they found me uninjured. I rather enjoyed the joke myself. The captain of the *Suviah* died of his disease a few months later, and I believe before the mutineers were tried. I hope they got clear, because, as before stated, I always thought the mutiny was all in the brain of a very weak and sick man.

After reaching shore, or Shell Island, the labor of getting to Corpus Christi was slow and tedious. There was, if my memory serves me, but one small steamer to transport troops and baggage when the 4th infantry arrived. Others were procured later. The distance from Shell Island to Corpus Christi was some sixteen or eighteen miles. The channel to the bay was so shallow that the steamer, small as it was, had to be dragged over the bottom when loaded. Not more than one trip a day could be effected. Later this was remedied, by deepening the channel and increasing the number of vessels suitable to its navigation.

Corpus Christi is near the head of the bay of the same name, formed by the entrance of the Nueces River into tide-water, and is on the west bank of that bay. At the time of its first occupancy by United States troops there was a small Mexican hamlet there, containing probably less than one hundred souls. There was, in addition, a small American trading post, at which goods were sold to Mexican smugglers. All goods were put up in compact packages of about one hundred pounds each, suitable for loading on pack mules. Two of these packages made a load for an ordinary Mexican mule, and three for the larger ones. The bulk of the trade was in leaf tobacco, and domestic cotton-cloths and calicoes. The Mexicans had, before the arrival of the army, but little to offer in exchange except silver. The trade in tobacco was enormous, considering the population to be supplied. Almost every Mexican above the age of ten years, and many much younger, smoked the cigarette. Nearly every Mexican carried a pouch of leaf tobacco, powdered by rolling in the hands, and a roll of corn husks to make wrappers. The cigarettes were made by the smokers as they used them.

Up to the time of which I write, and for years afterwards — I think until the administration of President Juarez — the cultivation, manufacture and sale of tobacco constituted a government monopoly, and paid the bulk of the revenue collected from internal sources. The price was enormously high, and made successful smuggling very profitable. The difficulty of obtaining tobacco is probably the reason why everybody, male and female, used it at that time. I know from my own experience that when I was at West Point, the fact that tobacco, in every form, was prohibited, and the mere possession of the weed severely punished, made the majority of the cadets, myself included, try to acquire the habit of using it. I failed utterly at the time and for many years afterward; but the majority accomplished the object of their youthful ambition.

Under Spanish rule Mexico was prohibited from producing anything that the mother-country could supply. This rule excluded the cultivation of the grape, olive and many other articles to which the soil and climate were well adapted. The country was governed for "revenue only"; and tobacco, which cannot be raised in Spain, but is indigenous to Mexico, offered a fine instrumentality for securing this prime object of government. The native population had been in the habit of using "the weed" from a period, back of any recorded history of this continent. Bad habits — if not restrained by law or public opinion — spread more rapidly and universally than good ones, and the Spanish colonists adopted the use of tobacco almost as generally as the natives. Spain, therefore, in order to secure the largest revenue from this source, prohibited the cultivation, except in specified localities — and in these places farmed out the privilege at a very high price. The tobacco when raised could only be sold to the government, and the price to the consumer was limited only by the avarice of the authorities, and the capacity of the people to pay.

All laws for the government of the country were enacted in Spain, and the officers for their execution were appointed by the Crown, and sent out to the New El Dorado. The Mexicans had been brought up ignorant of how to legislate or how to rule. When they gained their independence, after many years of war, it was the most natural thing in the world that they should adopt as their own the laws then in existence. The only change was, that Mexico became her own executor of the laws and the recipient of the revenues. The tobacco tax, yielding so large a revenue under the law as it stood, was one of the last, if not the very last, of the obnoxious imposts to be repealed. Now, the citizens are allowed to cultivate any crops the soil will yield. Tobacco is cheap, and every quality can be produced. Its use is by no means so general as when I first visited the country.

Gradually the "Army of Occupation" assembled at Corpus Christi. When it was all together it consisted of seven companies of the 2d regiment of dragoons, four companies of light artillery, five regiments of infantry — the 3d, 4th, 5th, 7th and 8th — and one regiment of artillery acting as infantry — not more than three thousand men in all. General Zachary Taylor commanded the whole. There were troops enough in one body to establish a drill and discipline sufficient to fit men and officers for all they were capable of in case of battle. The rank and file were composed of men who had enlisted in time of peace, to serve for seven dollars a month, and were necessarily inferior as material to the average volunteers enlisted later in the war expressly to fight, and also to the volunteers in the war for the preservation of the Union. The men engaged in the Mexican war were brave, and the officers of the regular army, from highest to lowest, were educated in their profession. A more efficient army for its number and armament, I do not believe ever fought a battle than the one commanded by General Taylor in his first two engagements on Mexican — or Texan soil. . . .

CHAPTER 2   Life Was Gay

Not all activities at Corpus Christi were military. Though boredom and sickness increased as months passed without action, the men found various ways to entertain themselves: some preferred to hunt or fish; others passed the time in bars, brothels, and gambling dens which sprang up around the camp. Lieutenant James Longstreet (1821–1904) of South Carolina, later a famous Confederate general, recalled what he and his friends did for amusement.

JAMES LONGSTREET
From Manassas to Appomattox:
Memoirs of the Civil War in America
Philadelphia, J. B. Lippincott Company, 1896, pp. 19–21

By the middle of October, 1845, three thousand eight hundred and sixty men of all arms had concentrated at Corpus Christi. Seven companies of the Second Dragoons had marched from Fort Jesup to San Patricio on the Nueces River, about twenty-eight miles up from Corpus Christi; the other three companies were halted at San Antonio, Texas. Near our camps were extensive plains well adapted to military manoeuvres, which were put to prompt use for drill and professional instruction. There were many advantages too in the way of amusement; game on the wild prairies and fish in the broad gulf were plentiful, and there was the salt water for bathing. On one occasion during the winter a violent north wind forced the waters over the beach, in some places far enough to disturb our camps, and when they receded, quantities of fish were found in the little puddles left behind, and turtles more than enough to supply the army.

The officers built a theatre, depending upon their own efforts to reimburse them. As there was no one outside the army except two rancheros within a hundred miles, our dramatic company was organized from among the officers, who took both male and female characters. In farce and comedy we did well enough, and soon collected funds to pay for the building and incidental expenses. The house was filled every night. General [William J.] Worth always encouraging us, General Taylor sometimes, and General [David E.] Twiggs occasionally, we found ourselves in funds sufficient to send over to New Orleans for costumes, and concluded to try tragedy. The "Moor of Venice" was chosen, Lieutenant Theodoric Porter [brother of the rear-admiral] to be the Moor, and Lieutenant U. S. Grant to be the daughter of Brabantio. But after rehearsal Porter protested that male heroines could not support the character nor give sentiment to the hero, so we sent over to New Orleans and secured Mrs. Hart, who was popular with the garrisons in Florida. Then all went well, and life through the winter was gay.

CHAPTER 3   War Has
                                             Commenced

After waiting seven months at Corpus Christi while American and Mexican diplomats negotiated unsuccessfully, Taylor's army moved south to the Rio Grande. Near the mouth of the river, opposite the Mexican city of Matamoros, the Americans built a fort, and soon the war began.

With Taylor's forces was New Yorker William S. Henry (1817–1851), an 1835 graduate of the United States Military Academy. " 'Taylor's Trail' will never be obliterated," wrote the twenty-nine-year-old first lieutenant.

LIEUTENANT   WILLIAM   S.   HENRY
Campaign Sketches of the War with Mexico
New York, Harper & Brothers, 1847, pp. 52–53, 64–86, 88–100, 103

MARCH 8TH [1846]. We are off for the Rio Grande! Colonel Twiggs, with the 2d Regiment of Dragoons, and Major Samuel Ringgold, with company of Horse Artillery, left at ten this morning; officers and men were in tip-top health and spirits, and all eager to reach our extreme southwest boundary. Old "Davy Branch," the major's trusty and beautiful charger, after gaining laurels on the turf, is equally ready to reap them on the battle-field, under his gallant and accomplished owner.

MARCH 9TH. The 1st Brigade, under General Worth, having with him [James] Duncan's battery, took their departure, and were followed on the 10th by the 2d Brigade, under Lieutenant-colonel [J. S.] McIntosh.

MARCH 11TH. The 3d Brigade (to which I was attached), under the command of Colonel [William] Whistler, with [Braxton] Bragg's battery, left their old stamping-ground. We were the first to arrive, the last to leave. General Taylor and staff left the same day. Corpus Christi looked perfectly deserted; the field of white canvas was no longer visible; the camp-ground looked like desolation itself; but the bright waters of the bay looked as sweetly as ever. The army were encamped upon its borders seven months and eleven days.

The day was oppressively hot. As we were quietly marching along, some commotion was created at the head of the column. It was caused by some of the men killing two piccarees (wild hogs); one of them, after being shot, made for the column, and was knocked down by one of the men with the butt of his gun; and a mustang, taking it into his head to be a little restive, relieved himself of his load, a demure-looking camp woman. After a march of sixteen miles, we encamped on the Nueces. . . .

*　*　*

MARCH 28TH. A day not easily forgotten. About eight A.M. we started for Matamoras, or, rather, the Rio Grande. Many believed that before we reached the river we would have a fight. I was, and have been, an unbeliever; however, we were all prepared, and I can not say but some would have liked a "brush" for exercise. The country passed over was really beautiful; such grazing was never seen before. The ground appeared alive with quail, and every water-hole turned out its flock of ducks. As you approach the river the chaparral increases in density. The soil is very rich. If they intended to attack us, numerous points could have been selected where they could have forced us into a bloody fight. Within a mile of the river we came to some settlements; large fields were inclosed by driving in posts and filling up the spaces with brush. The country is a perfect level, and the roads are in capital order. As we approached the bank we passed through a long line of Mexican huts: stopped at one, and there was a regular rush for *eggs and chickens;* salt grub for a few days gave us an appetite for *"chicken fixings."* The floor of the house was paved with bricks, and covered with beds. Not a dark-eyed lassie made her appearance. On one of the beds a small goat was sleeping, and under every one, and in every corner, a game-cock was tied by the legs. The domestic animals appeared to have "carte-blanche" to occupy the parlor with their mistresses. The poor devils at their cottage doors appeared pleased at our arrival, and saluted us as we passed.

We reached the river at 11 o'clock. The far-famed and much-talked-about waters rolled beneath us, and the city of Matamoras rose like a fairy vision before our enraptured eyes. I was so agreeably disappointed, I was inclined to grant it more beauty than it probably possessed. When we arrived some two hundred persons were on the opposite bank. The Mexican colors were flying from the quarters of the commander, General [Francisco] Mejia; from the Place d'Artillerie; and from the quarters of the Sappers and Miners. Those were the prominent places pointed out to us upon our arrival. Two of the advanced guard of the Dragoons, being some distance from the main body, were pounced upon by a body of Mexicans and carried off prisoners to Matamoras; a little bugler-boy was dismounted and his horse taken from him. This seizure caused no little excitement, and we were all ready to take the city at any risk.

General Worth was deputed by General Taylor to open communication with the commander of the Mexican forces, and bear to him an answer to the deputation which visited General T. at Point Isabel. Some time elapsed before the Mexicans would send a boat over. At last one came with an officer, to whom General Worth expressed his desire to see the commanding officer of the troops at Matamoras. The officer returned to General Mejia, who sent an answer to the effect that he would neither receive General Worth, nor the communication of General Taylor. He sent his second in command, General La Vega, to meet General Worth; the latter crossed the river, and the interview took place on the opposite side. General La Vega spoke of our arrival as an act of invasion; that the Mexican government looked upon it as such; and asked the question, "What would we have done if we had been served so?" Of course, no reply could be given, except that we would have fought like lions for what we deemed our possessions. They are decidedly inimical to us. General Worth did not touch upon the capture of the Dragoons, leaving that subject until a friendly intercourse could be established.

Two hours after our arrival a flag-staff was erected, under the superintendence of Colonel Belknap, and soon the flag of our country, a virgin one, was seen floating upon the banks of the Rio Grande, proclaiming in a silent but impressive manner that the "area of freedom" was again extended. As it was hoisted the band of the 8th Infantry played the "Star-spangled Banner," and the field music "Yankee Doodle." There was not ceremony enough in raising it. The troops should have been paraded under arms, the banner of our country should have been hoisted with patriotic strains of music, and a national salute should have proclaimed, in tones of thunder, that "Liberty and Union, now and forever, one and inseparable," had advanced to the banks of the Rio Grande. Simultaneous with the appearance of the "Stars and Stripes," the cross of St. George, and the French and Spanish colors, were run up from the different consulates. We looked in vain for ours: either our consul is confined, or else he dare not raise it. We have had no communication with him.

The main body of the city is half a mile from the river; scattering houses near the bank. From our position we can discover several strong-holds, and it looks as if it was well defended.

It is reported the different forts are well supplied with ammunition, and ordnance of heavy caliber. At this point the river runs nearly east and west, and is one hundred and seventy-five yards wide. The city is on the south side, and situated in an alluvial bottom. The soil is very rich, and of a similar character to that on the Mississippi. If the climate is not too dry, it must be immensely valuable. The river reminds one a good deal of the Arkansas, and the water is capital for drinking. The Mexicans expected we would have struck the river higher up, opposite their main ferry, where they are reported to be actively engaged in throwing up a work. I am convinced, if it becomes necessary for us to take the city, we can do it, although we have no siege artillery. They could not withstand such an onset as would come from us. General La Vega spoke to General Worth about raising our flag; he did not like it. I presume it looked like taking possession in earnest; one from which there will be no retreat. General Worth told him "it was a matter of taste, but that no sight was so glorious to him as that of the flag of his country floating in the breeze."

In the evening I walked down to the bank, and found it lined with citizens, attracted, no doubt, by the arrival of so many strangers. Strolling along, and seeing some genteel-looking young ladies upon the bank, I took off my hat and saluted them with "Buena noche, señoritas." They laughed most heartily, and appeared very much inclined to enter into conversation. The river at this point was so narrow that I could have thrown a stone across it. As our troops approached, the windows and house-tops were filled with citizens, anxious to see what we intended doing. Their troops kicked up a little dust by marching about some infantry and cavalry, of whom we caught glimpses through the trees; and, to finish the incidents of the day, a rooster, brought from Corpus Christi by Colonel T., the moment the wagon arrived upon the bank flapped his wings and crowed defiance. Our camp was in a corn-field, the corn some six inches high. General Taylor sent for the owner, and told him he would pay him what he thought was the value of

the crop. Rumor estimates the force of the Mexicans at one
thousand five hundred.

MARCH 29TH. The enemy, during the night, mounted a heavy
gun in a battery made of sand-bags, and this morning we had
the pleasure of reflecting that no little damage might be done
us, if they should amuse themselves by firing it. They are
missing a great deal of delightful society by behaving in so
churlish a manner. It is rather provoking being in sight of so
much comfort and luxury, without permission to enjoy it.
Fight or no fight, the general has made up his mind not to
budge from here, and has ordered Major [Joseph K. F.] Mansfield, of the Engineers, to make surveys, with a view of throwing up a work.

MARCH 30TH. Last evening we had quite an alarm. At tattoo
it was reported that, "from information received, there was a
strong probability of a night attack." Some Mexicans had
reported the crossing of a large body of the enemy's cavalry
above our camp, and it was thought their object was to attack
"Point Isabel," and at the same time open their batteries upon
us. I was among the unbelievers; yet it was impossible to divest
one's self of the thoughts of what *might* be the result, if the
premises were granted. The watch-word was given out, and
the men ordered to sleep upon their arms. Captain [Charles]
May, with a squadron of the 2d Dragoons, was ordered to
march to Point Isabel, a distance of *twenty-seven* miles, in *four*
hours, to re-enforce the garrison and put them on their guard.
With that officer's usual energy and promptness, he accomplished the distance in the stated time, and somewhat *stirred up*
the gentlemen with an idea of an attack. Morning dawned,
however; no gun was fired, no attack was made upon the depôt
at the Point. I then felt more satisfied that no contingency
could happen that would produce a fight. They had permitted
two golden opportunities to pass: the passage of the Colorado,
and the night of our arrival. Had they fired upon us the night
of the alarm, there is no computing the damage which would
have ensued. The train was placed in the center of the camp,

and if the firing had commenced, there would have been a "stampede" of some six hundred animals; they would have carried death and destruction with them. The return of killed and wounded by *mules* would have exceeded the number by Mexicans. A death by a *stampede* would have been a glorious finale for officer or man! I lay awake contriving how I should escape them, but my imagination could present no means, unless to "lie down and take it;" relying upon the faint hope that Mr. Mule would be military enough, considering his late education, to "*pass obstacle.*"

The enemy were hard at work all day, throwing up traverses to the sand-bag battery. Groups of well-dressed officers were lounging in front of it, and guards were passing to and fro. Their soldiers are in full uniform, and all have the Mexican blanket to protect them from the inclemency of the weather. Our situation is truly extraordinary: right in the enemy's country (to all appearance), actually occupying their corn and cotton fields, the people of the soil leaving their homes, and we, with a small handful of men, marching with colors flying and drums beating, right under the very guns of one of their principal cities, displaying the star-spangled banner, as if in defiance, under their very nose; and they, with an army twice our size *at least*, sit quietly down and make no resistance, not the first effort to drive us off.

MARCH 31ST. It is reported that the families of gentility are leaving the city. The weather is extremely disagreeable, and the Mexicans say we bring it with us. Walked up to the upper ferry to examine the work the enemy are constructing. It is called Fort Paredes, and is erected to command the passage of the river. At the landing we saw crowds of both sexes; the men were actively at work on the fort, and many of the women were washing. Nearly all the latter have well-developed, magnificent figures: they dress with as little clothing as can well be fancied, and appear as happy and contented as the day is long. They talked to me across the river, and asked "how we all were." I told them "well," and "hoped we were all friends."

They replied, "yes." I do not doubt it; and if these poor devils could decide the matter, it would all be settled. Two men swam the river and deserted.

APRIL 1ST. General Taylor having demanded the release of the captured Dragoons, they were returned to-day, with nearly all their equipments. This was another evidence of no very *actively* hostile feeling, but, as General Mejia, in his note, termed it, "one of great magnanimity." The whole city turned out to see the Dragoons when they were carried over the river prisoners, and the captors were looked upon as noble fellows, who had performed a deed of signal bravery. They were imprisoned, but treated with kindness. When the order for their return was given, there was a great deal of difficulty in finding their effects: it appears they were divided among their captors, and were to be kept as trophies. No doubt they gave them up with regret, as any article captured from the "barbarians of the North" must be of inestimable value in their eyes.

APRIL 2D. Order received settling the much-vexed question of brevet rank. General Worth, considering himself aggrieved by it, resigned. The enemy are still at work on a line of defenses; details from our men getting fascines and hurdles for our proposed work. Quite a military display among the enemy — seemed to have had a review. They have excellent music; there is one singularity, however, in it; at times, conspicuous above all sounds, you hear an everlasting bugle, deafening the ear with the same monotonous notes. Daily reports are received of their intention to give us battle: all agree that when General [Pedro de] Ampudia (rendered notorious by boiling Santa-manat's head in oil) arrives, then we shall "see sights," and nothing can hold him back from a fight. His proclamation, which has preceded him, styling us "barbarians of the North," &c., would cause the world to believe he intended to *eat us right up*, and make of us some delicate *man's head soup*. Our men appear to be very anxious for his arrival; a fight appears to be all they want, and I verily believe it is their nightly prayer.

APRIL 3D. Broke ground for a battery, to be erected in

advance of the main field-work. Several of the men have deserted; grand military display among the enemy. One of their regiments showed themselves, and looked very well. They have been actively employed every day in throwing up defensive works. The extreme work below the town was finished today, and a priest was seen consecrating it by sprinkling holy water over it.

APRIL 4TH. This afternoon a rapid discharge of musketry was heard below the camp, on the river bank. The first impression was, the enemy had made an attack. The long roll was beaten and the regiments promptly formed: the 1st Brigade, which was near the river, with a yell rushed to their arms. It was soon discovered the firing proceeded from our picket guard, and that it was at a man who attempted to desert by swimming the river. He was shot and sank. The Mexicans scampered from the bank, and thought we had commenced upon them. The whole affair was one of some little excitement, and proved with what alacrity our men would fly to their arms.

APRIL 5TH. Last evening the camp was again disturbed by the report of fire-arms. Another attempt at desertion, and another death. Four eighteen pounders arrived to-day.

APRIL 6TH. More of our men deserted last night. This morning our guns were placed in battery.

APRIL 7TH. Little or nothing done; the number of the enemy increasing.

APRIL 8TH. Broke ground upon the field-work. All the men off duty will be constantly employed until it is finished. Captain Mansfield has the direction of it. Some four or five of the deserters have been drowned in crossing the river. One man to-day succeeded in reaching the opposite shore, and as he crawled out the sentinel fired, and he fell dead. The Mexicans immediately covered him with a sheet and buried him. It was a capital shot for a musket, being about two hundred yards, and must give them no contemptible idea of our shooting. Three slaves of officers have run away. Of course every inducement is offered by the enemy. Major R.'s boy returned, and said he was treated with "the most distinguished consideration;" "had the first seat at the table, and the best bed in the house."

APRIL 9TH. We hear to-day Mr. [John] Slidell has left Mexico. After repeated attempts to open negotiations, he at last gave up all hope, and sailed for the United States the latter part of March, 1846.

APRIL 10TH. Colonel [Trueman] Cross left camp this morning, and, not returning in the evening, great fears are entertained for his safety: parties have been sent in every direction in search of him; and thinking he might be lost, General Taylor directed some cannon to be fired, to guide him to camp. I fear he is either a prisoner, or has been murdered.

APRIL 11TH. "Ampudia is coming!" "Ampudia is coming!" has been the daily cry. This morning a salute of twenty guns was fired, the church bells rang, the bands played, the troops paraded; and, true enough, Ampudia came. Nothing from Colonel Cross. Colonel [Ethan A.] Hitchcock, much to the regret of the army, from his wretched health, was forced to leave for the States.

A translation of an article from the *Matamoras Gazette* has afforded us no little amusement. It goes on to say, "There have been forty-three men desertions from the 'barbarians,' six slaves, and they expect momentarily *old Taylor, body and soul.*" When they do get him they will have a bitter pill to swallow.

APRIL 12TH. A dismal day; raining and very cold. The field-work vigorously pushed toward completion. About 2 P.M. a parley was sounded from the opposite side, and two Mexican officers crossed, and were escorted by Captain [W. W. S.] Bliss to General Taylor's tent. They remained but a few minutes, and returned. As Captain Bliss rode by a knot of us, warming ourselves by a small fire, he said, "Well, you may get ready; it's coming." Of course, we knew something serious had transpired, and that the impression at headquarters was, the long-expected fight was to come off — the ball to be opened. The officers bore a communication to General Taylor from General Ampudia. The general was told that "he must leave his position in *twenty-four hours*, retire to the Nueces, and there await the settlement of this question by negotiation: in default of which, Mexico would look upon his position as a declaration of war." He added, "The war should be carried on agreeably to the usages of the most civilized nations by him, and he hoped it would be so by us." Every disposition was made immediately to resist the threatened attack. Some believed that all the grace we were to have was "the twenty-four hours," and that at its expiration we must look out for shot. The 1st Brigade was immediately moved to the right, out of range. The general sent word to Ampudia that he did not require twenty-four hours, but would reply at 10 o'clock A.M. tomorrow. It certainly looks as if hard knocks were approaching. We have every confidence in the courage and patriotism of our general, and believe he will fight to the last.

APRIL 13TH. Early in the morning the 2d Brigade was moved to the left of the line, out of range of shot. General Twiggs, with the Dragoons and Ringgold's battery, occupied the center, and the 3d Brigade was moved into the interior of the field-work, together with Bragg's and Duncan's batteries. In this position the 3d Brigade were defiladed from the fires of the enemy, and the remainder formed a line so strong that the camp was considered impregnable. At 10 A.M. General Taylor's reply was sent over. It was mild, dignified, concise, and firm—perfectly characteristic of the man. He told General Ampudia, "He was sent here by order of his government, in a peaceable attitude, and *intended to remain;* and then warned him against the responsibility of firing the first gun." No guns were fired: the completion of the work was pressed forward.

Various rumors reached us this morning of the enemy having crossed in large numbers below. It is definitely understood that some have crossed. That is all we ask of them: cross and fight us, and we will exterminate them. The general is in capital spirits, and feels confident in the strength of his position. The 4th Infantry, 1st company of Dragoons, and [Major Samuel]

Ringgold's battery, were ordered to march immediately to meet the train coming from Point Isabel. It is thought those of the enemy who have crossed intend attacking it. We have heard nothing more of Colonel Cross: those most sanguine of his safety have given him up. He has undoubtedly been murdered by some of the bands of assassins who are roaming about the country. His unaccountable disappearance, and probable horrible fate, have cast a gloom over the camp. He was esteemed an excellent officer, one of more than ordinary attainments, and stood deservedly high in his profession. He was a high-minded, chivalric gentleman.

APRIL 14TH. The train arrived without being attacked, and Captain [Seth] Thornton returned reporting no signs of the enemy. At Matamoras every thing has been unusually quiet; hardly any citizens, and but few workmen, made their appearance; there was a solemn silence reigning over the whole city: it appeared to be deserted. It was impossible to explain it. It is now considered very unsafe to leave camp to go any distance.

The land in this vicinity is cultivated to some extent. Some of us occupy cotton fields, some corn. The soil is of the richest alluvial character, susceptible of the highest cultivation; for sugar it can not be surpassed. The whole valley of the Rio Grande, after the settlement of this question, must be rapidly and densely populated. In ten years this wilderness will "smile and blossom like the rose." How gorgeously rich the plantations will be on its banks! Nearly every thing grows here. In the vicinity of the camp there are the remains of a beautiful garden, and in it you have the orange, lemon, fig, banana, plantain, peach, and cocoanut. It had evidently at one time been under high cultivation, and ornamented with choice and beautiful flowers. This rich body of land is between thirty-five and forty miles in width, and some two hundred and fifty in length.

APRIL 15TH. The whole command at work on the fort. The enemy keep pace with us, and *shovel* sand in a style that can give us no contemptible idea of their proficiency in the use of that instrument. A rumor reached us that Ampudia has been superseded. Lieutenant Deas, of the Artillery, swam the river last night for the purpose, as he stated, of searching for Colonel Cross. General Taylor has blockaded the mouth of the river; the enemy are, therefore, cut off from receiving their supplies from New Orleans.

APRIL 16TH. About 11 o'clock four Mexican officers, in full dress, made their appearance; they were bearers of the reply of General Ampudia to General Taylor's letter concerning Colonel Cross. They have heard nothing of him; report Lieutenant Deas as a prisoner on parole.

APRIL 17TH. No change. Great military displays with the enemy, and a proportionate barking of dogs in the city. Lieutenant Dobbins of the 3d Infantry, and Lieutenant Porter of the 4th, each with a command of ten men and one non-commissioned officer, left camp with the avowed intention of catching, if possible, some of the band of the notorious Romano Falcon, hoping to discover some clew to the murder of Colonel Cross.

APRIL 18TH. Actually rained out of our camp, and were forced to remove it to the bank of the river. The sergeant of Lieutenant Porter's command came in and reported that the Lieutenant had been attacked by some Mexicans and was killed. His story is rather contradictory, and we await with great impatience the arrival of Lieutenant Dobbins, or some of the command, to confirm it.

APRIL 19TH. The corporal of Lieutenant Porter's party has returned, and confirms the melancholy report of yesterday. Lieutenant Dobbins separated from Lieutenant Porter, and was to meet him at a certain spot. About 2 P.M. on the 19th, met with a party of armed Mexicans engaged in jerking beef. As they approached their camp, a Mexican snapped his piece at Lieutenant Porter, who returned it with both barrels of his gun. The enemy immediately fled, and the lieutenant found himself in the possession of ten horses and twenty Mexican blankets. He immediately mounted his men and proceeded to camp. At this time it commenced raining violently. He had gone but a short distance when, near the edge of a dense chaparral, he was attacked by a party of Mexicans concealed therein. He ordered his men to dismount; the enemy kept up a brisk fire; both of the lieutenant's barrels snapped, and nearly all the pieces of his men had been rendered useless by the rain. One man by the name of Flood was shot down. After the lieutenant found his piece would not go off, he called to one of the men to hand him his musket; before he could get it, he was shot in the left thigh, and falling, said, "Never mind the gun! *Fight on, my boys! Take care of yourselves!*" The men being unable to get off their pieces, broke for the chaparral, became separated, and found their way into camp as they best could. The man who came in last says he concealed himself until dark in the edge of the chaparral, and saw the proceedings of the enemy. During the fight they yelled like Indians; as soon as our men broke they rushed upon the lieutenant and Flood: the latter they surrounded and deliberately knifed, and then performed the same inhuman office upon Lieutenant P. Lieutenant Porter was the son of the late commodore, and entered the army in 1838: he was a brave, gallant officer, and much esteemed in his Regiment. His fate is truly deplorable. Two commands were sent out to seek for his body. They were neither able to find it, nor the spot where the fight took place. All parts of the country are so precisely similar, and destitute of landmarks, that it is almost an impossibility to return to any one spot.

APRIL 20TH. Nothing new.

APRIL 21ST. A Mexican came into camp and reported he knew where the body of an American officer was lying. A command was immediately dispatched for it; it was recognized as being the remains of the lamented Cross; there can be no doubt of its identity.

APRIL 22D. General Ampudia wrote to General Taylor, "That he understood from undoubted authority the river was blockaded; that two vessels laden with stores for his army had been seized and carried into Brazos Santiago. He thought this blockade, under the present circumstances, was unauthorized by the law of nations, and requested him to raise it, or serious consequences would ensue." This is the amount of the communication. These *"serious consequences"* did not alarm us, for we are getting quite accustomed to their highflown language. The vessels spoken of were not taken, as represented by General Ampudia, but were warned off by our navy.

APRIL 23D. General Taylor replied to the communication received yesterday. It is a capital paper; truly republican, and American in every respect, and for which he should receive the approbation of the people. He is a man of sound views, and by his *strong common sense* (a pretty scarce article nowadays), is sure to arrive at a correct and just conclusion. We feel that the honor of the country is intrusted in safe hands. In his reply, he reviewed every thing which has occurred since we left Corpus Christi to this date; spoke of the proclamation he had issued prior to his departure, in which he said "he would protect the civil and religious rights of the citizens"; that it was with no hostile intentions he advanced to the Rio Grande; reminded him that a Spanish translation of that proclamation had been sent to Matamoras, and that he *knew* General Mejia had seen it; states that his advance was met twenty miles from the Colorado, and were warned, if they advanced, it would be considered a "declaration of war"; at the Colorado they threatened to fire upon him, and again repeated the "declaration of war;" that at Point Isabel he was met by a deputation from Matamoras, at the head of which was the prefect of the State of Tamaulipas, protesting against his occupying the country: after delivering the protest, they caused some buildings to be set on fire, which General Taylor deemed "an act of war." Opposite Matamoras he was again told that his occupancy of the country was looked upon as a "declaration of war." To all these declarations of hostile intentions no heed had been paid; no change had been made in our treatment of, or behavior toward them; but General Taylor had pursued the even tenor of his way. But when General Ampudia arrived, and gave General Taylor "twenty-four hours to quit," he deemed it time to turn his attention to the repeated threats, and conceives the "blockade of the river the least offensive act of war he could have committed under the circumstances; that the blockade had been reported to his government, and he should *maintain* it until he received their orders. Offers them an armistice until the question of boundary is settled, or war declared; and if that is accepted, will raise the blockade, but on no other terms." Tells them he can not pass over the objectionable style and tone of his (Ampudia's) correspondence; that the epithets of "usurpers," "invaders," &c., will not be permitted, and informs him, in future it must be more respectful, or it will not be received; and concludes by giving him his choice of action: that he is equally ready and prepared for peace or war. Affairs are approaching a crisis; they can not remain thus long. The enemy are reported short of provisions; they must either fight, treat, or just naturally dissolve themselves before many days.

A board of officers assembled to-day to report upon all the circumstances connected with the death of the lamented Cross. A Mexican reported the colonel was captured by Romano Falcon's band of *authorized murderers;* after taking him prisoner, they stripped him of every thing, and then consulted what should be done with him. The majority were for taking him over the river, when Falcon walked up and decided the matter by striking the colonel on his head with the butt of his pistol, from which blow he immediately died. There is no proof of this tale; but the hole in the skull was evidently made by the butt of a pistol.

APRIL 24TH. The remains of the late Colonel Cross were buried at half past 4 P.M. His escort was composed of a squadron of Dragoons and eight companies of Infantry, the whole commanded by Colonel Twiggs. The procession, under the circumstances, was painfully imposing. First came the Infantry, next the Dragoons, next the body, drawn by six horses, on the wheels of a caisson, enveloped in the flag of his country; next a sad mourner, his son; then a horse clad in mourning, led by two Dragoons, followed by all the officers off duty. The march was so conducted that part of the way it could be seen from the city; groups of soldiers and officers were upon the enemy's works, and on the bank of the river. The grave was dug at the foot of the flag-staff; the flag was at half mast. Colonel [Thomas] Childs read the service for the dead; three volleys were fired, the flag was run up, the escort marched off to a gay and lively tune, and left the dead in silence. Such is a military funeral: we have no time for grief.

APRIL 25TH. About 10 A.M. a grand review took place among the enemy; great military rejoicing; [General Mariano] Arista arrived. He communicated that fact in a note, couched in courteous and gentlemanly terms, transmitted to the general by one of his staff. In the afternoon reports reached us that the enemy were crossing the river, above and below, in great force. Captain Thornton was sent out in the evening with a squadron of the 2d Dragoons to ascertain the fact of their crossing above. Captain [William J.] Hardee and Lieutenants Kane and Mason were the officers of the party. Every one was on the "qui vive" to ascertain its truth, as, for several days past, matters were assuming a more hostile appearance.

APRIL 26TH. The camp was electrified by the news brought by Chapita, the Mexican guide who accompanied Captain Thornton. He returned, and stated Captain Thornton had an engagement with a large body of Mexicans, and all had been either cut to pieces or taken prisoners. The excitement which prevailed in camp can hardly be imagined: the report was passed from tent to tent, and an immediate engagement was thought not improbable. About 11 o'clock a wounded dragoon was brought in on a cart; he was sent by General [Anastasio] Torrejon, the commander of the force engaged with Captain Thornton, with a note to General Taylor, stating "that, on the score of humanity, he claimed the right of sending him two dragoons, wounded in the affair of to-day (26th), as he had no *flying hospital*; that the officers and men would be treated with all the rights of prisoners of war, by order of his chief." The man who was brought in had a very confused idea of the affair; knew that Captain Hardee was a prisoner, but was uncertain about the rest; reporting Captain Thornton and Lieutenant Kane killed. Increased activity was used in pressing forward the work; the general himself, for hours at a time, superintending it. All idea of there being *no fight* has ceased. *War has commenced,* and we look for a conflict within a few days. The train now at Point Isabel is ordered to remain.

General Taylor dispatched a messenger this evening with a requisition on the governors of Louisiana and Texas for five thousand men; three thousand from the former, two thousand from the latter. There is no doubt the enemy are crossing the river, and that all communication with Point Isabel is extremely hazardous. The troops sent for on General Taylor's requisition are expected to be used "to carry the war into Africa." We expect to *whip the Africans back to their country* before their arrival. In anticipation of an attack, the utmost vigilance is used at "the lines." An intrenchment has been thrown up around the camp, and the troops are lying in it under arms before daylight every morning.

APRIL 27TH. The general received Captain Hardee's report of the fight. He states that after the guide refused to go any further, on account of the proximity of the enemy, they advanced about three miles, and came to a large plantation surrounded by a very high chaparral fence; that the whole squadron entered the field through the open bars, and advanced about two hundred yards to a house. While there the alarm was given of the enemy. "Our gallant commander ordered a charge, and led it in person; they dashed toward the bars again, but found them occupied by a large body of Infantry. They dashed to the right, under a galling fire, to endeavor to find a passage." Captain Thornton here fell; and Captain Hardee, taking command, called on his men to follow, and dashed toward the river, intending to swim it, but found the banks too boggy. He returned and formed his men out of range of Infantry.

Perceiving they were completely hemmed in, he determined, if he could get honorable terms, to surrender; if not, to die fighting. He rode forward; met an officer; his terms were granted, and he surrendered his party, forty-five prisoners. He states "that Captain Thornton was unhorsed," and, "I hear, died in a personal conflict with Romano Falcon." "Lieutenant Mason was not seen, but died, no doubt, fighting gallantly." "The gallant Sergeant Tredor fell in the first charge, and Sergeant Smith was unhorsed and killed." They were taken to Matamoras. Captain Hardee and Lieutenant Kane live at the hotel of General Ampudia, eat at his table, and are treated with the greatest kindness. General Arista "received them most graciously," put them on half pay, and gave them a ration, or, in lieu thereof, twenty-five cents per day. On Captain Hardee's declining, for himself and Lieutenant Kane, to receive the half pay, and requesting permission to send for some money, he refused, stating he would take the best of care of them. He speaks in high terms of their kind treatment. It was certainly unexpected, and is highly creditable to the enemy.

APRIL 28TH. This morning a report was received from Captain Thornton: the gallant fellow is safe, and is uninjured, save a slight contusion from the fall of his horse. His horse (the "old roan," who had carried him through the Florida war) was shot, and fell on him. He was discovered by some of the enemy some time after the battle had ceased, taken prisoner, and carried into Matamoras. Poor Mason, it appears, is the only officer killed. He was the nephew of Colonel Mason of the 1st Dragoons, and graduated from West Point in 1842; was assigned as a brevet to the 1st Dragoons, and promoted to the 2d. He was universally beloved; a high-toned, chivalric, and withal a very modest officer; recollections of his noble traits of character will ever be fresh in our memories. Two sergeants and eight privates were killed. It was a complete ambuscade; the nature of the country rendered it impossible for them to have discovered an enemy; in the densely thick chaparral any number of men could have remained concealed.

The force of General Torrejon is estimated at two thousand five hundred. General Canales is reported to be in our vicinity. Captain G. A. M'Call, 4th Infantry, with one hundred picked men, was sent out to obtain information of the enemy. Captain Walker has authority from General Taylor to raise a company of volunteers. Those he has already enlisted have been stationed midway between this and the Point. Captain Walker has been for some time identified with the border struggles of Texas, and was one of the unfortunate Mier prisoners. Early this morning his camp was attacked by the enemy. He had left fifteen of his men, and gone on a scout with the remainder. Five of his men were killed and four are missing. One of the men was evidently *lariated*, and was probably choked to death before he was pulled off his horse. Generals Canales and Torrejon are supposed to have been in command of the attacking force, and Colonel Quintaro is reported to have his arm broken.

APRIL 29TH. It is reported that the Mexicans had attacked Point Isabel, and were signally defeated by Major Munroe, with his two companies of Artillery. The report was too good to be believed; but when Captain McCall returned in the evening, and reported he had heard the discharge of artillery in the direction of the Point, it became generally credited. Every preparation is being made to march to the Point. Subsistence and other stores removed into the fort, wood cut and hauled, &c.

APRIL 30TH. The 7th Regiment of Infantry, under the command of Major [Jacob] Brown, have been designated by the general to remain at the fort; Bragg's battery, and Captain Lowd, with his company, in charge of the eighteen-pound battery, constitute the remainder of the garrison. The report of the attack upon Point Isabel was erroneous; the impression gains ground that we will be attacked on our march.

MAY 1ST. The general decided we should march at 4 P.M. Every preparation had been made to meet the enemy, and we marched at the appointed hour in capital spirits. We passed through the chaparral without meeting any of the enemy. The march was continued until 12 o'clock at night, and one of the most fatiguing I have ever endured. We slept under arms in the broad prairie, without any fires to take off the chill of the night air. The march was resumed on the 2d, and we reached the Point at 12 o'clock, having suffered much from the intense heat and want of water.

*　　*　　*

Before reveille on the morning of the 3d of May, 1846, the heavy, booming sound of cannon came rolling in from the direction of the fort, opposite Matamoras. The camp was wild with excitement; we knew our gallant fellows were resisting a bombardment, and all were anxious to fly to their rescue. Captain Walker, on a scout last evening, after taking a survey of the enemy's camp, fell in with their picket guard and fired upon them. He reports the enemy in force, and evidently awaiting our return. We were under orders to march at 1 P.M., but the general changed his mind, and decided upon communicating with the fort. Captain May, with a command of Dragoons, was ordered to accompany Captain Walker (who was selected by the general to carry his communication to the fort) as far as the edge of the chaparral, and, if he did not return before morning, to wait no longer, but return to the Point. We were kept in a constant state of excitement; the firing continuing at intervals the whole day.

On the morning of the 4th, Captain May returned, having waited as long as he deemed it prudent for Captain Walker. He reports fresh signs of the enemy. Early in the morning we had an exciting *scare:* the cry was the "enemy are advancing." The long roll was beaten, troops paraded, and immediately marched out to meet them. The "enemy" was Captain May and his command. The 1st Brigade, which was encamped two miles in advance of the Point, after the alarm moved to our present camp, situated on an extensive flat running along the bay. Active preparations are making for our return march, and for leaving *Fort Polk* in a defensible state.

Captain Walker returned on the 5th, and brought the cheering intelligence that all was well at the fort. The batteries from the city were opened upon the fort at daybreak on the 3d. In thirty minutes all fires from the heavy gun batteries were silenced by the superior skill of our artillerists. The enemy have continued throwing shells, but with trifling effect. The reception of such good news put us in the very best spirits. Captain Walker ran a great many risks making his way to the fort, and deserves great credit for the fearless manner in which he effected the communication. The heavy report of artillery throughout the day announces the bombardment in continuance. Little was done on the 6th but to make preparations for the coming march. On the 7th, General Taylor issued the following order:

Headquarters, Army of Occupation,
May 7, 1846
Order No. 58.

The army will march to-day at 3 o'clock, in the direction of Matamoras. It is known the enemy has recently occupied the route in force. If still in possession, the general will give him battle. The commanding general has every confidence in his officers and men. If his orders and instructions are carried out, he has no doubt of the result, let the enemy meet him in what numbers they may. He wishes to enjoin upon the battalions of Infantry that their main dependence must be in the bayonet.

Signed,
W. W. S. BLISS,
Assistant Adjutant-general.

The order, in advance, announced a victory. There was no doubt expressed in it. Commanding a much inferior force, composed of troops few of whom have ever "smelt gunpowder," our brave general, nevertheless, speaks to them as to old veterans. He *wishes the Infantry to recollect their main de-*

pendence must be in the bayonet. That sentence alone shows
the man; in it you see confidence, and a determination to win
the battle at all hazards. The army marches at 3 p.m., having
in company an immense train, rich, not only in subsistence, but
in munitions of war. In the wagons there were six twelve-
pounders. There was also with us a battery of two eighteen-
pounders drawn by oxen, the command of which was assigned
to Lieutenant Churchill, of the Artillery. We marched five
miles and encamped.

Early on the morning of the 8th our scouts under Captain
Walker reported the camp of the enemy deserted. From that
it was generally believed they would decline battle. The march
was resumed shortly after sunrise. Upon our arrival within a
short distance of our last camp, previous to our reaching the
Rio Grande, the advance reported the enemy in force. De-
bouching from a point of mesquite, the masses of the enemy
were apparent, less than a mile distant, and occupying a front
of nearly a mile and a half. The general immediately had his
command formed in column of attack, and with the greatest
deliberation ordered arms, and permitted the men, half at a
time, to go and get water to fill their canteens. We had already
marched twelve miles, the day was very warm, and we had
suffered from the want of water. As soon as the men had re-
freshed themselves, the command was formed, and marched
steadily to meet the enemy, with as much regularity and coolness as if on drill. Two squadrons of Dragoons were at first in
advance, but, after the battle commenced, were employed
either gallantly supporting the batteries, or defending the train.
When within seven hundred yards, the enemy opened their fire
from a battery on their right. The column was halted, and
deployed with the utmost precision, except the 8th Infantry,
which remained in column during the action.

The following was the order of our line of battle: The right
wing, commanded by Colonel Twiggs, was composed of the
5th Infantry on the right, Ringgold's Artillery, the 3d Infantry,
Churchill's eighteen-pound battery, and 4th Infantry. Left

wing, commanded by Brevet Lieutenant-colonel Belknap, composed of Duncan's Artillery — the Artillery companies serving
as Infantry — and the 8th Infantry. Ringgold's and Duncan's
batteries were immediately advanced and opened their fires.
The firing of the enemy was incessant, although not very ac-
curate. The enemy's line of battle was along and in advance of
the chaparral. Their cavalry (Lancers) were on the left, then
a battery, then masses of Infantry, then a battery, masses of
Infantry, another battery, and again masses of Infantry. Their
position had been deliberately assumed, knowing where we
would pass the road. The fire of the gallant Ringgold's battery
on our right told with deadly effect upon their mass of Cavalry;
platoons appeared to be mowed down at a time. The two
eighteen-pounders carried death and destruction with them.
The Cavalry soon found it was getting too warm for them, and
commenced moving off, by a flank movement, to the left in a
trot, and were *tickled* into a gallop by a discharge of the eighteens. Their flank movement threatened our train, and was
promptly met by the movement of a section of Ringgold's battery under Lieutenant [Randolph] Ridgely, the 5th and 3d
Infantry. The strength of this body of Cavalry was computed
at one thousand, and, therefore, was a formidable demonstration. The 5th received them in square, and from the fire of an
angle vacated twenty saddles. Some of them still passed on,
until they saw the 3d advancing in column by division, when
they rapidly retreated. Lieutenant Ridgely performed excellent
service with his pieces. He aimed and fired a shell, which
struck a lancer about the middle, which exploded simultaneously with the blow, making one mangled mass of horse and
rider. Thus the battle progressed on our right. On the left, the
gallant Duncan was pouring in a most destructive fire. Each
shot seemed to take effect, and as our men saw the execution,
their cries of triumph mingled with the cannon's roar. The fire
of the enemy upon our left was more galling; the 8th Infantry,
particularly, suffered, having been kept in column, instead of
being deployed in line. The Regiments of Artillery and Infan-

try, and squadrons of Dragoons, stood firm as veterans, ready to support our batteries. The prairie took fire, and the burning of the long, rank grass sent up columns of smoke, which at times concealed the opposing forces. The cannonading commenced at 3 P.M., and ceased for a short time at 4 P.M.

In the mean time, a masterly movement to the right, to out-flank the enemy, was being executed. Ringgold's battery and the eighteen-pounders were pushed forward toward the left flank of the enemy. The 4th Infantry and 1st Brigade moved up to their support. As soon as the firing recommenced, the enemy were forced to change their line of battle. Lieutenant Duncan, under cover of the smoke, conceived and executed a brilliant flank movement on the enemy's right. He advanced with his battery, and suddenly debouched and poured in a galling enfilading fire upon their right flank; it was thrown into the utmost confusion. His shells and shrapnell shot told with murderous effect. At this moment, if a charge had been made, so great was the confusion of the enemy, the whole field would have been swept; but the general felt bound to protect his train, and feared any movement which would have laid it open to an attack. As night approached the fire of the enemy slackened, and it ceased on both sides with the setting sun. We had driven the enemy from his position, and forced him to retire. We encamped as victors upon the field of battle. The last rays of the setting sun tinged with a golden light the clouds of battle that hung heavily over the field of carnage; the weary army rested on their arms, and slept sweetly on the prairie grass. Our loss was wonderfully small. Nine killed, forty-four wounded, and two missing. Major Ringgold, Captain Page, Lieutenants Luther, 2d Artillery, and Wallen, 4th Infantry, were wounded. Major Ringgold received a shot while seated on his horse, which carried away the flesh on his legs from his knees up, and passed through the withers of his thorough-bred charger, "David Branch"; Captain Page had his lower jaw shot off; Lieutenant Luther was wounded in the calf of the leg, and Lieutenant Wallen very slightly in the arm; Captain Bliss, assistant

adjutant-general, had his horse shot under him; likewise Lieutenant Daniels of the 2d Artillery. The wounds of the men
were very severe, most of them requiring amputation of some
limb. The surgeon's saw was going the livelong night, and the
groans of the poor sufferers were heart-rending. Too much
praise can not be bestowed upon our medical officers for their
devotion and prompt action. It was a sad duty for them. The
enemy, commanded by General Arista, were six thousand
strong; we were two thousand two hundred and eleven; only
the difference of three thousand one hundred and one, and they
in a selected position. Singular to relate, the battle of Palo Alto
(tall timber) was fought on the spot which General Taylor
predicted when he first passed over the ground.

At daybreak on the 9th the enemy were seen moving along
the edge of the chaparral toward the road, and the prevailing
impression was that they intended occupying the road in force,
and disputing our further progress. The general determining to
advance and attack decided to park the train, throwing up a
temporary breastwork, and mounting some of the twelve-
pounders for its defense. Shortly after sunrise the army was
again formed in line of battle, and marched forward. The
wounded were left behind to be sent to Point Isabel. The Dragoons and Captain Walker's company of Volunteers, thrown
out in advance, soon returned and reported the chaparral free,
and the enemy in full retreat along the road. The army was
halted near a pond, and General Taylor rode back to the train
to send off his first bulletin, to cheer the desponding at home,
and to awaken American glory and patriotism. While there,
Lieutenant Blake, of the topographical corps, accidentally shot
himself. It was a sad occurrence; he had behaved with distinguished gallantry on the 8th. I took advantage of the halt to go
over the field of battle. It was truly a shocking sight; our
Artillery had literally *mowed* them down. There were heaps
of dead lying hither and yon, with the most ghastly wounds I
ever saw; some had died with a smile on their countenance;
others, in the agony of death, with a fierce convulsive struggle

had caught at the rank grass, and died with their hands clinched firmly in it, looking defiance at the enemy. It was a shocking picture. The number killed could not be accurately ascertained, but of killed and wounded we are safe in claiming five hundred. The great disproportion in the loss of the two armies arose from this fact: *we fired at their masses; they at our batteries!* The prisoners taken acknowledge they were badly whipped, and confirm us in the belief of the strength of their army.

As we were advancing we came across a poor fellow who was wounded, and who, without a drop of water, had passed the night upon the battle-field. He gave us to understand he wanted bread and water. Colonel Twiggs exclaimed, "Men, give this poor fellow something to eat and drink." In an instant the haversacks and canteens of a company were at his service. Such acts of generosity threw a flickering sunbeam over the deep shades of the battle-field. On the field was found a dog lying by the dead body of his master; no entreaties could prevail upon him to leave the body of him who in life had caressed him. General Taylor ordered out parties in every direction to search for the wounded of the enemy, had them brought in, and attended to with the same care as our men.

About 1 P.M. the army resumed its march. When we first halted, Captain G. A. McCall had been sent in advance, with one hundred picked men, to scour the chaparral and watch the progress of the enemy. Captain C. F. Smith, of the Artillery, with his battalion of light companies of the 1st Brigade, followed. We proceeded through the chaparral to within three miles of the fort, when word was passed to the rear that the enemy were in force, and in a selected position. The advance under Captain McCall had discovered them, and after a spirited brush, retired, agreeably to orders, to await the arrival of the main body. There was not a moment's hesitation; our brave general determined to give them immediate battle. Our troops filed past the train, and deployed as skirmishers to the right and left of the road. Captain McCall's command was ordered by the general "to advance and draw the fire of the enemy." Nobly did they perform that terrible service.

The enemy occupying the opposite bank of a ravine, concave toward us, had planted their batteries to rake the road, and every approach (few in number) through the almost impenetrable chaparral. The fire of the enemy was drawn by the advance. Lieutenant Ridgely, fit successor to the gallant Ringgold, was ordered forward with his battery. The struggle for victory then commenced. The Artillery of the enemy swept the ground with their grape and cannister; Lieutenant Ridgely returned it with murderous effect. Masses of their Infantry, lining the banks of the ravine, and pressed forward into the chaparral, were met by our skirmishers on the left with a gallantry and determination, on both sides, rarely equaled. Repeatedly were bayonets crossed, the enemy giving way slowly, and fighting for every inch of the ground. The 4th, 5th, 8th, and part of the 3d were on the left, and engaged in this sanguinary struggle. Owing to the dense chaparral, the Regiments became mixed, but fought not the less severely. The enemy clung to their batteries with the greatest pertinacity. Ridgely's Artillery thundered in reply. This gallant officer, in one of his daring advances, had only one piece unlimbered, when he was charged by a body of lancers, who came dashing down upon him like thunder, when Sergeant Kearnes put a load of cannister on the top of a shell and fired it; this scattered them all but *four*, who still dashed along. Lieutenant Ridgely charged them in person, and drove them off.

Captain May rode back to the general, and asked if he should charge the battery on the opposite side of the ravine. *"Charge, captain, nolens volens!"* was the reply; and away dashed the gallant fellow. As he passed Ridgely's battery, Ridgely exclaimed, *"Hold on, Charley, till I draw their fire!"* and it is well for May that he partially succeeded. Away dashed this gallant squadron down the ravine; Lieutenant Inge fell, and many of their saddles were vacated. On went the rest; crossed the ravine, and captured the battery. Captain Graham's company was associated with May's in this memorable charge. General La Vega, standing at his battery to the last, was taken prisoner by May, and passed to the rear.

On the right of the road, where the 3d deployed, no enemy was met; but the Regiment so far outflanked them as to be in danger of fires from our own batteries. The density of the chaparral was such that they could not make their way through, but were forced to return, in order to get into the action. They reached the ravine just after the desperate charge of the Infantry (in which the 8th was so conspicuous) had completely routed the enemy. Immediately after their batteries were captured, Duncan came up with his battery and took the advance. The Dragoons, 3d Infantry, and Captain Smith's command were ordered to support the Artillery. The enemy were in full retreat. On we all pushed, hemmed in a narrow road by a dense chaparral on each side, the Artillery advancing and pouring in its bloody fire, and clearing the road. About two hundred yards from the ravine we came upon the camp of the enemy. It was already captured and deserted. To this point the gallant [Captain Philip] Barbour had fearlessly advanced with his company of the 3d Infantry, and, unaided, successfully resisted a desperate charge of cavalry: the empty saddles, and horses writhing in the agony of death, marked the spot where the struggle occurred.

The huge packs of the enemy were arranged with great regularity upon the ground; mules, some with packs, were scattered about; beeves were killed, their camp-fires lighted, and their meals cooking. They evidently expected to have been undisturbed that night. On, on we went, keeping up a run, and yelling like mad! The enemy now and then gave symptoms of a stand, but were driven on, scattering themselves in the chaparral, and availing themselves of every trail that led to the river. We neared the lines of our old camp; our cheers reached high heaven, when they were suddenly silenced by three shots from an eighteen-pounder which came very near killing some of our men. The first impression was that our friends had mistaken us for the enemy, and were firing at us from the fort; but we soon ascertained the shots came from the city.* The enemy fled in every direction, and many were drowned in their attempts to swim the river. It was a perfect rout, "horse, foot, and dragoons."

Our brave general had gained a glorious victory over the best-appointed army Mexico ever sent into the field; confident of success, in an almost impregnable position, and with an overwhelming force, at least three to one. There were two thousand troops not in the battle of the 8th, who crossed the river the evening of that day, expressly to join in the battle of the 9th. They were veterans of *twenty* successful battles, and in their own country, upon whichever side they fought, victory perched. Every thing was in their favor; position, numbers, confidence; and, yet, with all these, they failed. History does not furnish a more striking battle than "Resaca de la Palma," the battle of the 9th of May. So confident were they of victory, that Ampudia, speaking to Captain Thornton, who was then their prisoner, said "it was utterly impossible that it could be otherwise; that their numbers alone were sufficient, independent of those *veteran* regiments." General La Vega said that "if he had any sum of money in camp, he should have considered it as safe as if at the city of Mexico; and he would *have bet any amount that no ten thousand men could have driven them.*" The dead, dying, and wounded were strewed in every direction. Our brilliant victory was purchased with the blood of some gallant souls.

Our loss in this action was three officers and thirty-six men killed, twelve officers and fifty-nine men wounded. . . . We captured from the enemy, eight pieces of artillery, two thousand stand of arms, two hundred mules, a great number of packs and the necessary appurtenances, all the baggage and camp

---

* The Artillery Battalion, under Colonel Childs, remained in rear to guard the train, and thus reduced our fighting force to one thousand seven hundred.

equipage of the army, and one hundred and fifty thousand rounds of musket cartridges. All General Arista's private baggage and papers fell into our hands, from which much important information was obtained. One general, one colonel, one lieutenant-colonel, four captains, and five lieutenants were taken prisoners. Three captains and four lieutenants were buried on the field; and they acknowledge that forty-eight officers, besides these, are missing. The loss of the enemy in killed, wounded, and missing can not be less than two thousand. It was a victory achieved by the *army proper*, and, as such, doubly dear to us.

Many acts of individual daring are recorded. General Taylor was sitting on his horse in the thickest of the fight, with his sword drawn, while the balls were rattling around him. Colonel C., the amiable sutler of the 4th Infantry, formerly mayor of Augusta, Ga., and well known for his courage and kindness of disposition, remarked to him that he was exposing his person very much, and proposed to him to retire a short distance: "*Let us ride a little nearer, the balls will fall behind us,*" was the general's reply. Lieutenant Lincoln, of the 8th, killed two Mexicans with his saber.

It is a great pity we were unable to follow up our success. Had we crossed the river the night of the battle, Matamoras would have been ours without a blow; as it is, we may have to fight for it. It was with feelings of deep regret we heard, upon our arrival, of the death of Major Brown, the commanding officer of the fort. He was struck in the leg by a shell, on the 6th of May; amputation became necessary; but from confinement in a bomb-proof, and debility arising from excessive fatigue and watching, his system could not rally. He died a few hours before the cry of victory reached him. He was a brave and gallant soldier, and the general knew full well into whose hands the defense of the fort was intrusted. The bones of every man would have been piled up in it before he would have surrendered. He has earned for himself, and the regiment to which he belonged, a glorious reputation, which must be shared with Lowd's and Bragg's batteries. Captain Hawkins, of the 7th, the next in rank, assumed command when Major Brown was wounded. The defenders of the fort have suffered every thing; they have been harassed night and day, and all looked haggard from the want of sleep. From the morning of the 3d to the afternoon of the 9th of May, they were subjected to an incessant bombardment. The enemy completely invested them, and established three batteries, producing a cross-fire upon the work. General Arista summoned them to surrender, representing to them there was no chance of General Taylor's coming to their succor. It was promptly and most positively declined. The enemy had fired at them some two thousand seven hundred shells and shot, killing one officer, one sergeant, and wounding thirteen privates. Their small loss can hardly be credited; a special Providence seemed to have intervened to preserve them from destruction. . . .

CHAPTER 4   Ready for
Peace or War

After its initial victories, Taylor's army occupied Matamoros
for several months while preparations were made for the next
operation. The Americans, augmented by volunteer units and
supplies, started for Monterrey, some two hundred fifty miles
southwest of Matamoros, in the summer of 1846. Instead of
taking the most direct route over arid land, Taylor decided to
go up the Rio Grande to Camargo and then follow the San
Juan Valley south. Lieutenant Henry described the occupation
of Matamoros and the march to Monterrey.

LIEUTENANT WILLIAM S. HENRY
Campaign Sketches of the War with Mexico
New York, Harper & Brothers, 1847, pp. 118, 123, 156–159, 164

The good citizens [of Matamoros] are becoming more at
home with us; many of the genteel classes are showing themselves. There is a great deal of beauty among them — some
most strikingly beautiful faces. They lead a luxurious life, at
least I call it so; and if any of my readers have inhabited a
southern clime, and felt the enervating effects of the climate,
they will agree with me. They sit all day long in buildings
with thick walls and brick floors, with their beautiful suits of

hair nicely braided and tied up, having the least quantity of dress you can *possibly* fancy; and in the evening they emerge like bees from their hives, take possession of their balconies, and enjoy one of the most delicious evening climates that God has ever granted poor mortals. I apply this, of course, to the better class, for the filth of the other is not endurable. They are very sociable, and will permit you to stop at their lattice windows and gaze on their beautiful faces, whether from sheer laziness, or love of admiration, I will not pretend to decide. If you are a lover of nature — *unadorned* — you can gratify your taste by walking up to Fort Paredes any pleasant evening, and witness the fair ones bathing in the Rio Grande; no offense is taken by looking at them enjoying their aquatic amusements.

The river has risen to an immense height, and in many places overflown its banks. It will be quite favorable to our operations, provided the rise does not subside before our boats arrive. Lieutenant-colonel Payne is ordered to Washington, to convey the standards and other trophies taken from the enemy. Our wounded are generally doing very well, except Captain Page, who, it is thought, can not recover.

Early in July our steam-boats commenced arriving. The 7th Infantry, under the command of Captain Miles, left for Reynosa, on their way to Camargo, on the 6th and 7th of July. These companies took water transportation, and the remainder started to march. They were compelled to relinquish the prosecution of it by the back-water from the river, and were forced at last to take water transportation. For many years such a freshet has not been known. It is a mighty current. The Mexicans say there has been a special interposition of Divine Providence in our favor, causing the river to rise so that we can transport our troops and supplies to Camargo without any trouble. If they really think so, the omen must be any thing but favorable to their cause. It certainly never was intended this lovely land, rich in every production, with a climate that exceeds any thing the imagination can conceive of, should remain in the hands of an ignorant and degenerate race. The finger of Fate points, if not to their eventual extinction, to the time when they will cease to be owners, and when the Anglo-American race will rule with republican simplicity and justice, a land literally "flowing with milk and honey"; who will, by their superior mental, if not physical abilities — by their energy and *go-a-head-a-tiveness*, which no sufferings or privations can retard, which shines alike in the frozen regions of the North and under the burning sun of the South, render available the surprising fertility of the soil, its immense mineral wealth, and populate the country with a race of men who will prove the infinite goodness of our Maker in creating nothing but what is for use and some good purpose.

No part of Texas surpasses in fertility, or equals in salubrity, the Valley of the Rio Grande. The river courses its way from the mountains through a varied climate, which will produce any thing, from wheat to sugar and cotton. Nothing can exceed the rich growth of vines. The melon flourishes, and our camp is daily supplied with fine watermelons. This region of country is bound to be settled very rapidly; if nothing else points it out as a desirable location, the fact of the Rio Grande being *really a navigable* stream is sufficient. In point of health, few regions can surpass it. There are no causes for disease; there are no swamps, which, in the heat of summer, throw out their poisonous miasma; the banks are high, and the country preserves that character of the Colorado. Let this boundary be settled, and there will be a tide of emigration to this favored region rarely equaled. If some of our northern farmers would settle here, they could make one flower-garden of the river banks, from its source to its mouth. Cultivation can be carried on by white labor, I think, beyond a doubt. No summer climate can exceed it in loveliness; the everlasting breeze deprives the sun of much of its heat. Such evenings! Such a morn! Young people should come here to make love; the old should emigrate and rejuvenate themselves.

. . . Two of the Catholic clergymen, appointed chaplains to the army, have arrived. These appointments will be productive of much good. The Mexicans have been told they would be persecuted "for conscience sake"; that we would tolerate no religion but the Protestant; and their priests have added all the fuel to the flame they could, to produce the impression among these poor, ignorant creatures that we are a set of savage barbarians. Our acts, both civil and military, and now religious, will prove the contrary, and will open their eyes to the magnitude of the attempted deception.

The behavior of our army after victory is as highly honorable as the victories themselves. In taking possession of Matamoras we have not interfered with either the civil or religious rights of the inhabitants. Their courts of justice are still held, the most perfect respect is paid to law and order, and every infraction of either is severely punished. The army, instead of entering the city as conquerors, encamp quietly in the suburbs. Instead of taking possession of their houses for our men, we remain under *miserable* canvas, which affords no protection from the storm, and scarcely shade to protect the soldier from the noonday sun. Many have *no tents*, and yet, under these circumstances, no building is occupied: those taken for storehouses and public offices are regularly rented. By such conduct we have restored confidence to the people; the citizens mingle freely among us, walk through our camp, and feel sure of protection. Such conduct should make our countrymen proud of their army.

. . . Captain Duncan reports the military are actually lariating the "peones" into service; they will be used in throwing up fortifications at Monterey. From all the reports, we have to conclude great efforts are being made to resist us; and large levies of men, such as they are, are being collected. We are all delighted the advance has commenced, and are equally ready for peace or war: in one hand we hold the olive branch, in the other the sword. Let Mexico take her choice. In any event, under all circumstances, she may rest assured the latter will force her to take the former. For the sake of humanity, I hope her choice will be the former.

We received information of a revolution in Mexico; that General Alvarez had overthrown Paredes and taken him prisoner. That looked more like peace than any event that had occurred. When the subject of peace is advanced, the question invariably arises, "With whom are we to negotiate?" The President of to-day is a prisoner to-morrow; his views and intentions are totally changed in that brief period by a successful military aspirant seizing the reins of government. Were ever a poor, wretched people so situated? Was ever a duplicate of such a government known in the world? I really think there is a *dim* light of peace breaking through the darkness. God grant it! Although my profession is that of arms, and we may gain glory and honor by the exercise of it, yet I can not help thinking it would be more honorable and satisfactory to the people and the government to have this war brought to a speedy and peaceable termination. Then, again, the question arises, With whom *are we to treat?* If we make a treaty, what assurance have we it will be respected for a day? View it in any light, I see a long series of trouble and annoyance on this frontier.

A rumor comes to us that Colonel [William S.] Harney, with a mixed command of Dragoons and Texans, has left San Antonio on an expedition into the interior. General Twiggs, with four companies of Dragoons, Ridgely's and Taylor's batteries, arrived to-day. The latter battery is assigned to Worth's division. Every one is now purchasing mules. The transportation is so limited, that most of the officers have purchased one to carry along some few comforts. Our attempts at speaking Spanish are truly amusing; talk it you must, in some shape or other, or you fail making your bargain. The laughable attempts we make remind me of an anecdote which I heard at Corpus Christi. A man by the name of Clifton, a vagabond "leg," had lost his horse; going to look for him in the chaparral, he met a Mexican upon a similar expedition. Thinking he might be of service to him, he accosted him with:

"Look here, my man, have you seen anything of a d—d *caballo*, a *barnosing* about here, with a *cabrista* on his neck?"

"No entiende, señor."

"Don't understand! Why, the d—d fool *don't know his own language!*"

. . . The volunteers, as they landed at the Brasos, were forced, before moving into the interior, to encamp upon that barren, sandy island. The sand drifts in such clouds, you stand not only a chance of swallowing more than a man's allotted share, but of becoming blind likewise. A volunteer who thought he had swallowed his full share of it, thus accosted the doctor:

"I say, doctor, have you any thing that will remove a *sand-bar?*"

"No, sir."

"Well, then, I am a *gone sucker.* I've got a sand-bar in my innards, upon which every thing grounds, and I can't get any thing up nor down."

The volunteers continue arriving by every boat. They have suffered a great deal at their encampments near the mouth of the river. Diarrhoea, dysentery, and fevers have been very fatal. They must suffer much more than the regulars, for they have no idea how to collect around them those nameless comforts the old soldier always has; besides, campaigning is entirely out of their line; and my only surprise is, that people so suddenly transported from a high to a low latitude, in the middle of the summer, should have so few cases of disease. They may consider themselves very fortunate.

. . . We are passing one of the very best natural roads in the world, where, with very little repairs, wagons can always pass. Independent of the comfort and luxury of a wagon, and the fact that, with them, you can suit the hour of your march to the temperature of the day, no inconsiderable expense might be saved by their use. Eleven wagons (fifty-five mules) would have transported the command; whereas we have one hundred and twelve mules for the transportation of the baggage, at an expense of fifty-five cents per day. To say the least, it is the most *provoking* transportation we have had in any of our marches. The brigade was accompanied by four camp women;

one of them had gone to the expense of a Mexican lady's side-saddle, certainly one of the most curious specimens of saddlery I have ever seen. The lady sits square in the saddle, from which, in the place of a stirrup, is suspended a board, large enough for both feet; it has the usual horns, but much higher, and the back and sides are inclosed by vertical pieces of leather, often beautifully worked with silver thread. I do not think it would suit our fair equestriennes.

CHAPTER 5   Go It, My Boys

By mid-September 1846 Taylor's troops had reached Monterrey. The city was protected by strong forts, an army larger than Taylor's, and mountains on three sides. It looked impregnable to nearly everyone but Taylor. The old general elected to divide his army into two parts and to attack. This decision shocked many young graduates of the United States Military Academy who had been taught at West Point never to divide their forces when facing an enemy. If Taylor had heard of such a rule, it did not impress him. He favored raw courage — his own and his troops' — over military theory. Lieutenant Henry left a vivid account of the action at Monterrey.

LIEUTENANT   WILLIAM   S.   HENRY
Campaign Sketches of the War with Mexico
New York, Harper & Brothers, 1847, pp. 186–198, 200–209, 212, 216–219

. . . SEPTEMBER 16TH. From a Mexican, taken last night, the general squeezed out the following information: There are nine thousand men at the city, six thousand rancheros and three thousand regulars. The latter are the remains of the army we whipped on the 8th and 9th of May; the former swear they will not fight, and the latter they will. This little town can boast of most lovely scenery. The valley through which the river flows is quite level, covered with a rich growth of grass, affording ample grazing for any number of cattle. The mountains spring up directly from its plain; to the west, three passes opening through the mountains are striking features in the landscape, as viewed from town. The sunset this evening was gorgeously beautiful. This valley is capable of supporting an immense population, and ere long its banks will teem with rich harvests. This country comes nearer the idea of *fairy-land* than any of which I have ever conceived an opinion. All the good people of the north must think of it as such, for it *really* is so; and then they can people it and dress it up to suit their fancies. I will only add, if you give your imagination the rein, you will barely realize it. General Worth, with the 2d Division, arrived to-day. General [James P.] Henderson, with his command of Texas cavalry, is expected to-morrow, unless they have decided to follow the example of the Rifle Regiment, and take their discharge.

SEPTEMBER 17TH. Early in the morning I rode up to town for the purpose of making a minute examination of it. Fortunately, I found the Cathedral open, and ascended a spiral stair-case, inclosed in a masonry tower, upon which the belfry rests. I soon emerged upon the top. The view was magnificent, but, owing to the unusually hazy atmosphere, not as distinct as could have been desired. Before this elevated view I had no conception of the breadth of the Valley of the San Juan; it can not be less than fifteen miles. At the base of the mountains, to the south-west, I could distinctly see Monterey. I was surprised, for I had no idea it was visible; and then it looked so near, I could not credit it was twenty-five miles distant. The Bishop's Palace looked like a fortified place, and the city appeared to cover a great deal of ground; of course, every thing was very indistinct, yet very interesting, as all our hopes are at present concentrated upon that spot.

. . . The camp has been full of all sort of rumors — first fight, and then no fight. A reputed deserter made his appearance, fresh from the trenches, and reported there was no doubt we would be resisted — that the most extensive preparations were made; thereupon the *fightites* rose; then, again, a report contradictory of the former, and the fever would subside. In the evening, General Taylor received a communication from the Spanish consul at Monterey, asking whether the property of foreigners would be respected. The general replied, he could not be responsible for any thing if the city was taken by assault. General Ampudia has distributed along the road a printed proclamation, calling upon the men and officers of our army to desert, and stigmatizing the war as anti-Christian. He offers them protection, good pay, and equal rank in the Mexican service. How ignorant he must be of the character of the American soldier to think, for a moment, his offer could provoke other than a feeling of disgust. The volunteer division, under General [William O.] Butler, arrived to-day. Captain Craig was relieved from the pioneers, the road being good ahead. The order for the march is out; we move to-morrow morning. In case line of battle is formed, Twigg's Division will be on the right, the Volunteers in the center, and Worth's on the left.

*   *   *

SEPTEMBER 18TH. The first division of the army marched at 8 o'clock; the others followed, with an hour's intermission. The scenery was similar to that already described, save the ground was more rolling than it appeared from Marin. The valley is made up of gentle undulations, broad, level plains; the whole backed by huge mountains, whose cliffs are of a pink color in the morning's sun. The water of the San Juan was very cold, and wading it at early dawn was not very agreeable.

Eight miles from Marin passed a small stream called Agua Frio. Its banks were high, bottom rocky, some slate formations visible, and I have no doubt coal could be found. Quite a number of houses, I suppose the cabins of the peones attached to the hacienda, lined the banks. The "lord of the manor" had, for this country, quite a showy and extensive establishment. In his court-yard was seen one of those old Spanish coaches, heavy enough for six mules, and capable of containing a whole family. Its *tout ensemble* proved the owner a man of some pretensions. An Irishman, upon seeing it, exclaimed, "Och, but we're gettin' into civilization! Be Jabers! there's an *omnibus!*" A good many of the inhabitants came out to see us.

About three miles beyond the Agua Frio we reached the hacienda San Francisco, where we encamped. Just as our advance entered, the cavalry of the enemy left, and were in sight when we turned off to take our camp-ground. Many thought the enemy were in front in force, and a battle would ensue immediately; but it turned out to be the same force which has preceded us since we left Ceralvo. The Padre of the place told General Taylor that Ampudia would defend the place until death, and that it was well fortified. If we do fight, the Infantry will have to do the work, as our deficiency in heavy guns will render our field batteries almost useless. Some of the arrieros attempted to *stampede* today, but Colonel [H. L.] Kinney, with his usual energy and promptness, prevented them. They were alarmed, having heard that the bugbear, Canales, was in their rear. The alarm arose from General Henderson's Brigade, consisting of two mounted regiments of Texans, under the command of Colonel [Jack] Hays and [George] Woods, who joined us this evening. They are a fine body of men, and add some eleven hundred to our force.

SEPTEMBER 19TH. Marched at sunrise. General Henderson, with his brigade, and two companies of Rangers, in advance. General Taylor and staff accompanied them, to reconnoiter the place. Passed several plantations, and luxuriant fields of corn and sugar-cane. Marching slowly along, within three miles of the city, about 9 A.M., the report of a large cannon, re-echoing from mountain to mountain, told us most plainly the work had commenced, and that the enemy intended to make, at least, a show of fight. Two more reports, in quick succession, followed, and our men, from lagging behind, were inspired with a new energy, and pushed forward with increased vigor. They were ready for the fierce combat at the moment. Two more guns were fired, and the command was halted. The general and staff were seen slowly returning. It appears, when the advance presented themselves, some Lancers came out from the city, hoping, no doubt, our cavalry would charge upon them, when, as they came within range of their guns, many would be sacrificed. General Taylor saw through their design, and ordered a halt; and then it was the enemy opened upon them. The firing was from the citadel, some distance in advance of the city, and from guns of twelve pounds caliber. The third shot ricochéd and passed directly over the general's staff, coming very near him. The troops were immediately encamped about three miles from the city, in a magnificent grove of pecan and live oak. From the sides of the slope issue *springs* of water, which are said to be *streams* at their fountainhead.

After the general retired, the mounted troops remained some time in the vicinity of the spot where they were first fired upon. Several shots were fired at them with no effect. Of course, all is anxiety and excitement — storming parties — taking batteries — crossing ditches — all the subjects of conversation. A reconnoissance was immediately ordered, under charge of our engineer officers, and they are firing away at them with their big guns. As soon as it is finished the general will form his plans, and then we will know what work is cut out for us. The city appears well fortified; and their heavy guns give them a great advantage over us, our small pieces being of no use in battering down their walls. All we have to do is to *take theirs*, and use them against themselves! The greatest enthusiasm prevails among men and officers, and a perfect confidence of success is expressed. In our ignorance of its fortifications, no idea can be formed of the time that will be consumed in taking it; but the general impression is, that the struggle will be fierce, but soon over.

SEPTEMBER 20TH. Major Mansfield, in charge of a reconnoitering party, escorted by Captain [Archibald] Gillespie's company of Rangers, left yesterday at 4 P.M. to reconnoiter the works to the west of the town. He returned at 10 P.M., having reached within five hundred yards, when he was fired upon with grape. The whole party was repeatedly fired upon. He thinks the works on the heights above the palace quite strong, but that they can be carried by assault without much difficulty. Reconnoissances are actively going on. General Taylor decided upon sending General Worth with his division to take possession of the Saltillo road, and storm the heights to the west of the city. The division marched at noon in capital spirits. To this division was attached Colonel Hay's regiment, and Captains McCullough's and Gillespie's Rangers. The remaining divisions are left for the work in the plain and on the east of the city. The spot upon which we are encamped is called Walnut Grove, and is said to be a fashionable rendezvous for the exclusives of Monterey. A more charming spot for a pic-nic could not possibly be desired.

The works which command the approaches to the city appear to be as follows: on the west, the bishop's palace, and a fort on a height commanding it; to the north, the citadel, a regular bastion-work; and to the east, several detached redoubts: the streets are said to be barricaded.

At 4 P.M. one regiment from each brigade of the 1st and Volunteer Division, with Ridgely's, Bragg's, and Webster's batteries, were ordered out into the plain to make a diversion in favor of General Worth. General Taylor and his staff were out, and we presented quite an imposing appearance. The troops and the surrounding scenery made quite a striking picture. We thought we could trace by the dust the course of Worth's column. A fire was kept up at the train from the height above the bishop's palace. During the afternoon a battery was commenced for the mortar. After dusk some shots were fired at us and the working party. After dark all the troops retired but the 3d Infantry and Bragg's battery; they remained until 9 o'clock to cover the erection of the mortar battery. They were relieved by the 4th Infantry and the 1st

Regiment of Kentucky Volunteers, who remained upon the field all night. The mortar and two twenty-four-pound howitzers were established during the night, and will probably open upon the city in the morning.

SEPTEMBER 21ST. During the night an express was received from General Worth, stating he had arrived in position, and would storm two heights to the southwest of the castle before storming the height directly west of it. About 7 A.M. the 1st and Volunteer Divisions were ordered under arms, and advanced toward the city. The mortar and howitzer batteries opened, but with little or no effect. General Taylor directed the 1st Division to be moved toward the east of the city to support Major Mansfield in a close reconnoissance of the enemy's works. The division (owing to the indisposition of General Twiggs, who had no idea the action was to be brought on, and was at first in camp, but immediately repaired to the field) was under the command of Colonel Garland, 4th Infantry. The 4th Infantry, under Major Allen, being at the mortar battery, the division went into action with the 3d Infantry, commanded by Major Lear, the 4th Brigade, commanded by Colonel [Henry] Wilson, consisting of the 1st Infantry, commanded by Major Abercrombie, and the Baltimore Battalion under Colonel Watson, and Bragg's and Ridgely's batteries. Major Mansfield was directed by General Taylor to bring on the action, if he thought the works could be carried. The reconnoitering party was first supported by Company C., 3d Infantry, under the command of Lieutenant Hazlitt, and re-enforced, upon application, by Company H., 3d Infantry, under the command of Captain Field.

The division was formed in line of battle out of reach of the guns of the enemy, when orders were brought for us to advance (by Lieutenant [John] Pope, topographical engineer, and Colonel Kinney, who was acting as volunteer aid-de-camp), make our way into the city, and storm battery No. 1, at the extreme eastern end. As we advanced, battery No. 1 opened upon us. The first shot fired struck immediately in front of our line and ricochéd over it. An enfilading fire was opened upon us from the citadel. The line steadily but rapidly advanced, regardless of all fire; important work was to be performed, and we had made up our minds to carry all before us at the point of the bayonet. For five hundred yards we advanced across a plain under fire of the two batteries. We rushed into the streets. Unfortunately, we did not turn soon enough to the left, and had advanced but a short distance when we came suddenly upon an unknown battery, which opened its deadly fire upon us. From all its embrasures, from every house, from every yard, showers of balls were hurled upon us. Being in utter ignorance of our locality, we had to stand and take it; our men, covering themselves as well as they could, dealt death and destruction on every side; there was no resisting the deadly, concealed fire, which appeared to come from every direction. On every side we were cut down. Major Barbour was the first officer who was shot down; he fell, cheering his men. He was killed by an escopet ball passing through his heart. He never spoke; his most intimate friend, standing by his side, never received one kind look — one "God bless you!" but his spirit, in the twinkling of lightning, winged its way to his Maker.

We retired into the next street, under cover of some walls and houses. Into this street the body of Major Barbour was carried. Here were lying the dead, wounded, and dying. Captain Williams, of the topographical corps, lay on one side of the street, wounded; the gallant Major Mansfield, wounded in the leg, still pressed on with unabated ardor, cheering the men, and pointing out places of attack. It was in this street I saw the gallant Colonel Watson, followed by a few of his men (some of them were persuading him to retire). Never shall I forget the animated expression of his countenance when, in taking a drink from the canteen of one of his men, he exclaimed, "Never, boys! never will I yield an inch! I have too much Irish blood in me to give up!" A short time after this exclamation he was a corpse. Lieutenant Bragg's battery arrived about this time. He reached the street into which we had retired, but it was impossible for him to do any thing. Finding the struggle at this point hopeless, our force originally having been deemed only sufficient to carry battery No. 1, without any expectation of finding some two or three others raking us, we were ordered to retire in order, with the view of attacking the battery at a more salient point. In the mean time, Captain [Electus] Backus, of the 1st Infantry, succeeded in stationing himself, with some fifty men, in a tan-yard, which was about one hundred and thirty yards in the rear of battery No. 1, and nearer the town; in this yard was a shed, facing battery No. 1: its roof was flat, encompassed by a wall about two feet high, which was an excellent breast-work for his men. About twenty yards to the southwest of the battery was a large building, with very thick walls, used as a distillery. On the top of this building sand-bag embrasures had been constructed, and it was occupied by the enemy. The gorge of battery No. 1 was open toward the shed. Captain Backus, with his men, drove the enemy from the distillery with considerable loss. About this time he received information that we had been ordered to retire. Our firing having ceased, he was about withdrawing, when he again heard firing in front of the battery, and at the same time all the guns of the battery opened in the direction of the fire. This was the advance of *two* companies of 4th Infantry, about ninety strong, upon whom the fire of the enemy's batteries were concentrated, and actually mowed them down. It was actually *ninety* men advancing to storm a work defended by *five hundred!* It was here the gallant Hoskins and Woods fell, bravely cheering their men, and the generous Graham was wounded. Backus determined to retain his position; reposted his men on the roof of the shed, and shot down the enemy at their guns, firing through the open gorge of the work.

At this time the Mississippi and Tennessee regiments, under the command of General [John A.] Quitman, advanced under a very heavy fire, and gained possession of the battery, after a very severe loss. The galling fire of Backus saved many of their

gallant men. The greater part of the enemy had been driven
from the work before it was taken possession of by the command of General Quitman. Major-general Butler was wounded
in the leg while leading, in company with General Hamer, the
1st Ohio Regiment. In retiring from the city, we were exposed to a galling fire from the citadel. A ball took a man's
head off, and threw it and part of his gun high in the air.

When the division re-formed our terrible loss became apparent. In the 3d Infantry, its gallant commander, Major Lear,
was severely wounded by a ball entering at his nostril and coming out at the back of his ear. Lieutenant D. S. Irwin, adjutant
of the 3d Infantry, was killed by a shot in the neck. Captain
G. P. Field was killed by Lancers while retiring. Lieutenant
Hoskins, of the 4th Infantry, Lieutenant Woods, of the 2d
(serving with the 4th), were killed, and Lieutenant Graham
mortally wounded. Major Abercrombie, of the 1st Infantry,
was slightly wounded; Captain La Motte was shot in the arm;
Lieutenant Dillworth had a leg shot off; Lieutenant Terret was
wounded and taken prisoner. The division was then ordered to
the captured work to support Ridgely's battery, about being
ordered into the city.

During this time the mortar and three twenty-four-pound
howitzers were playing upon the city; one of them, having been
taken to the captured work, was now firing into Fort Diablo.
While under cover of the battery, we were ordered to enter
the city immediately, and carry, if possible, a work of the
enemy apparently but a few streets off. The command which
went on that fearful expedition was chiefly made up from the
3d and 4th Infantry. The moment we left the cover of the
work we were exposed to a galling fire of musketry, escopets,
and artillery. We pushed steadily along, taking advantage of
every shelter to approach the work. Captain L. N. Morris, 3d
Infantry, led the column. Crossing one street, we were exposed
in full to the guns (mounted in barbette) of a tête de pont,
which commanded the passage of El Puente Purissima. The
fire from it was perfectly awful. We advanced through several

gardens and streets, and at last worked our way to a spot where we were slightly sheltered from the shower of lead. The enemy had occupied these houses, and were driven from them by the determined advance of our men. We could not proceed any further, having arrived at an impassable stream, on the opposite side of which the enemy were in force with three pieces of artillery, from which an incessant fire was kept up on us. In fact, every street was blockaded, and every house a fortification; and on all sides our gallant officers and men were shot down. Our command did not number over one hundred and fifty, and the enemy were at least a thousand strong at the bridge. It would have been madness to storm it with a force so inadequate.

It was at this point that Captain L. N. Morris, while bravely leading his regiment, received a mortal wound; the shot passed through his body, killing him immediately. Going into action with five seniors, at this critical moment the command of the 3d Infantry devolved upon myself. Captain Bainbridge had been wounded in the hand just after leaving the captured battery. A few moments after Captain Morris fell, Lieutenant Hazlitt, of the 3d, received his death-wound. Here it was that the undaunted courage and bravery of the American soldier showed itself. Although exposed to a deadly fire, they would advance by file, assure themselves of their aim, fire, retire and load, and *again return* to the spot where the balls were flying thick and fast. At one time a whole regiment, coming to reenforce the command already at the bridge, was exposed to the fire of our men: it was very effective.

Major W. Graham was the senior officer of the 4th Infantry with this advanced command. The enemy being strongly reenforced, our cartridges nearly exhausted, the command was ordered to retire. This was done coolly and calmly, under (if possible) an increased fire. On arriving near the captured battery the command was forced to lie down flat in the road, under cover of a very small embankment of an irrigating ditch, for more than an hour, exposed to an incessant fire of bullets, ball, and shells, until ordered to take position under cover of the captured work.

Lieutenant Ridgely, with a section of his battery, advanced to the street leading to the "tête de pont," and fired several rounds, but, finding they were perfectly useless, his pieces were withdrawn. Lieutenant Bragg, with his battery, put to flight some little show of a charge of Lancers. Captain Shivers, with his company, did good service. The volunteers were all ordered to camp, excepting the 1st Kentucky, which was not in the action, having been kept as a guard over the mortar. They, with the 1st, 3d, and 4th Infantry, and Captain Shivers's company, were ordered to remain, to hold the captured work.

Just before dark an express arrived from General Worth stating that he had been successful in taking two heights, and would storm the one commanding the Bishop's Palace to-morrow at day-dawn. There was a smile of satisfaction passed over our good general's face, and when it was announced to the command we gave three cheers. A traverse was immediately thrown up, under the superintendence of Lieutenant Scarritt, Engineers, as a cover from the fire of the citadel. The 3d Infantry, with two companies of the 1st Kentucky Regiment, occupied the battery, the balance the distillery and houses in the neighborhood. The night set in cold, and, to complete our misery, it rained; the men had neither dinner nor supper, and, without even a blanket, were forced to lie down in the mud. Battery No. 1 mounted five pieces: one twelve-pounder, one nine, two sixes, and one howitzer.

While such were the operations under the immediate eye of General Taylor, General Worth, with his division, was moving for the Saltillo road. A large body of cavalry and some infantry disputed his further passage. The charge of the cavalry was met by the battalion of light troops under Captain C. F. Smith, and Captain McCullough's company of Rangers. The enemy charged by squadrons, and had to turn the foot of a hill before reaching our men. On they came, our men standing like rocks, and many a saddle was emptied by their unerring aim.

The first squadron was completely mixed up with our advance, when on came the second. Lieutenant Hays, of Duncan's battery, unlimbered the guns in a minute, and poured in round shot over the heads of our men. This dispersed the whole body, and the cry was, "*Sauve qui peut!*" In this sharp engagement, the enemy, it is presumed, lost one hundred, the colonel among the number.

As soon as the cavalry had retired, the enemy (from "Independence Hill," west of the Palace) opened upon our column a fire from a twelve-pounder. Under this fire the division marched two miles, incurring very little, if any loss. Out of range of this height, another battery of one gun opened from a hill, called "*Federacion*" (between these heights the road to Saltillo runs), and continued the fire until the division marching on the Saltillo road were out of range. At this point General Worth decided to storm the battery on Federacion Hill. Captain C. F. Smith, 2d Artillery, was selected, with about three hundred men, half regulars, and the rest Texans, under Major Chevalier, for this service. After the departure of Captain Smith, Captain Miles, with the 7th Infantry, was ordered to march to his support. His orders required him to take a direct route to the hill, through a cornfield, which would afford him slight shelter.

The advance of Captain Miles was unobserved by the enemy until he had nearly reached the small stream (the Arroyo Topa) which runs south of the city, and courses its way along the base of the hill upon which the battery was situated. As soon as the head of the column debouched, a discharge of grape was opened upon them, without injuring a man. Before crossing the river, two more discharges of grape were received, and the Infantry stationed upon the hill commenced a plunging fire — not a man was injured. As the regiment crossed the river, it was formed under a point of rock, out of reach of the enemy. Detachments were then sent forward under Lieutenants Grant, Little, and Gardner, to keep the enemy employed, and divert their attention from the advance of Captain Smith.

About this time Colonel Smith, commanding the 2d Brigade, arrived, with the 5th Infantry, and ordered Captain Miles, with the 7th, to follow that regiment in an attack upon Fort Soldado, a temporary breast-work on an eminence to the southeast of Federacion. As the brigade moved on, it was discovered that Captain Smith, with his command, had possession of the height. The 2d Brigade formed in line within four hundred yards of the redoubt, and rapidly advanced. It received one discharge of grape from a twelve-pounder, and *not a few* escopet balls; several were wounded. The advance continued rapidly until within a hundred yards, when the charge was made at double quick. The enemy fled in every direction.

In this affair the left wing of the 7th entered the redoubt with that of the 5th. There were also many of Captain Blanchard's gallant company of Louisiana Volunteers and Texan Rangers well up with the advance, each and all striving for the post of honor. Colonel Smith immediately made the following disposition of his command: Captain Smith to retain possession of the first height stormed; Captain Miles, with the 7th, to hold the last height taken; and Captain Scott, with the 5th Infantry, to move on the same ridge, further east. In this position the 2d Brigade remained during the afternoon and night of the 21st; the 7th Infantry receiving, for several hours, the fire from the Bishop's Palace, which was returned by the captured gun under charge of Lieutenant Dana, of the 7th Infantry. Soon after dark, General Worth communicated with Colonel Smith, informing him that at daybreak the next morning he intended storming the height above the Bishop's Palace, and that Captain Miles, with three companies of the 7th, must move in the direction of the Palace, to create a diversion.

SEPTEMBER 22D. Let us return to the eastern extremity of the city, where the command occupying battery No. 1, as soon as day dawned, were forced to lie flat down in the mud to cover themselves from the spiteful fire from Fort Diablo, which was incessantly kept up. Just at the gray dawn of day, lying on my back, I witnessed the storming of the height which commanded the Bishop's Palace. The first intimation we had of it was the discharge of musketry near the top of the hill. Each flash looked like an electric spark. The flashes and the white smoke ascended the hill side steadily, as if worked by machinery. The dark space between the apex of the height and the curling smoke of the musketry became less and less, until the whole became enveloped in smoke, and we knew it was gallantly carried. It was a glorious sight, and quite warmed up our cold and chilled bodies.

Firing commenced on us as soon as the day cleverly dawned. Many shells were thrown from the citadel, none of which burst in the work, although they fell all around us. Lieutenant Scarritt was busily employed putting the battery and distillery in a better state of defense. Captain Bainbridge assumed command of the 3d Infantry in the morning. The 1st, 3d, and 4th Infantry, and Kentucky regiment were relieved by a command under General Quitman, of Colonel [Jefferson] Davis's Mississippi regiment. Returning to camp, we were exposed to a cross and enfilading fire from the enemy's batteries. A corporal of the 4th Infantry was cut in two, and one man wounded. We had to scatter along to prevent being fired at in a body. The division were delighted to reach their camp, to have one night's rest. We had hardly arrived when an express came in, stating that General Worth had carried the castle, and another, from whence, I presume, will never be known, that the enemy were coming out to meet us in the plain! We were again immediately under arms, and marched out; no enemy appearing, we returned. At sunset the regiment followed to the grave the remains of the lamented Morris.

At daylight on the 22d, as I have previously mentioned, the attack was made upon the height commanding the Bishop's Palace, by a command under Colonel Childs, composed of artillery and infantry, and some Texans under Colonel Hays. At the moment the storming party commenced the ascent, the command under Captain Miles descended toward the palace, giving three cheers to attract the attention of the enemy; in return for their cheers, they received a shower of grape. This movement held the enemy in check at the castle, and prevented him from succoring his flying forces on the hill above, which was carried with great gallantry and slight loss. Captain Gillespie fell mortally wounded, the first man to enter the breastwork. Soon after, General Worth ordered up the 5th Infantry, Captain Smith's command, and Captain Blanchard's company of Louisiana Volunteers, to re-enforce Colonel Childs. With great exertion, a howitzer was placed in position, under charge of Lieutenant Roland, which played with a plunging fire upon the castle with great precision and effect. A light corps under Captain Vinton, composed of artillery, Blanchard's company and Texans, on the left of the hill, kept up a continued fire of musketry, which was returned with spirit by the enemy.

About noon the Mexican cavalry deployed before the palace, and made an attempt to charge our skirmishers. They were repulsed, and pursued closely by Vinton's command, preventing many from again entering the castle, rushing in themselves through every opening, and driving the enemy with consternation before them. Lieutenant Ayers was the first to enter and pull down the flag of the enemy, and run up the star-spangled banner. Great credit is due to Captain Vinton for his gallantry. General Worth, after the castle was taken, moved down all his forces and ammunition train from the ranch of the Saltillo road, and so remained during the night of the 22d, directing the 5th Infantry and Blanchard's company to return to the redoubt on the hill, where the 7th was stationed.

SEPTEMBER 23D. From our camp we had the pleasure of hearing General Worth open upon the town from the castle about 7 o'clock. A report was circulated that the enemy were attempting to escape. The whole command was immediately under arms, and marched almost within range of the enemy's guns. So many commanding points were in our possession, that we were momentarily in expectation of their capitulation. It was cheering to see Worth pouring it into them, and that, too, with their own pieces and ammunition. The rapid discharge of small-arms at the eastern end of the city gave notice that the engagement had again commenced. The regiment of Texas cavalry under Colonel Woods had dismounted, and, with the Mississippians, under Colonel Davis, were sharply at work. The Mississippians at daybreak took possession of Fort Diablo (from which we had received such a destructive fire on the 21st and 22d), without any resistance, the enemy having abandoned it, taking with them their guns during the night. General Quitman was in command. These troops fought most gallantly, driving the enemy before them from house to house, their rifles picking them off wherever a Mexican's body or head presented itself.

Bragg's battery was ordered into the city, and the 3d Infantry was ordered to support it. When we got within range of the guns of the citadel, the battery crossed the field of fire at full gallop; not one was injured. The 3d took a more circuitous route, and came up under cover. When we arrived the city had been cleared of the enemy on a line with, and within two squares of, the Cathedral, which is situated in the main Plaza, and in which they had been concentrated. General Quitman, General Henderson, General Lamar, Colonel Wood, and Colonel Davis all displayed distinguished gallantry; several of their men were wounded, and some few killed. Bragg's battery and the 3d Infantry dashed in among them, and shared the fight for the remainder of the day. The firing was very severe, but nothing compared to that on the 21st, except at one street running directly from the Cathedral. To cross that street you had to pass through a *shower* of *bullets*. One of Bragg's pieces played up this street with very little effect, as the weight of metal was entirely too light. Sergeant Weightman, Bragg's first sergeant, worked his piece like a hero, and was shot through the heart while aiming his gun. The Mexicans, whenever the piece was pointed at them, would fall behind their barricade, and at that time we could cross without a *certainty* of being shot; as soon as it was fired, their balls (as if bushels of hickory nuts, were hurled at us) swept the street. Our men crossed it in squads. "*Go it, my boys!*" and away some would start; others would wait until the enemy had foolishly expended at space their bullets, and then they would cross.

General Taylor was in town with his staff, on foot, walking about, perfectly regardless of danger. He was very imprudent in the exposure of his person. He crossed the street in which there was such a terrible fire in a walk, and by every chance should have been shot. I ran across with some of my men, and reminded him how much he was exposing himself, to which he replied, *"Take that ax and knock in that door."* When we commenced on the door the occupant signified, by putting the key in and unlocking it, if we had no objection, he would save us the trouble. It turned out to be quite an extensive apothecary-shop. The proprietor, Doctor San Juan (there are more St. Johns in this country than stones), was a very respectable-looking Esculapius, and offered us some delicious, ripe limes and cool water. I took some of the former, but declined the latter, as it was hinted it might be poisoned. One of the men, not so sensitive, made himself a *governor* lemonade, and told me it was *"first rate,"* and advised me to take some. The doctor said Ampudia was in the Plaza with four thousand men, and that two thousand were in the citadel. The house on the opposite corner had been broken open. It was a grocery store; in it the men found bread and other edibles. Bursting open another door, we came upon five rather genteel-looking women, with some children, and one or two men. They were on their knees, each with a crucifix, begging for mercy. As soon as they saw me, the cry was, "Capitano! capitano!" I reassured them by shaking hands, and, by the expression of my countenance, signified there was no danger. They appeared very grateful to find their throats were not to be cut. Although we are fiercely fighting, and the blood of our officers and men has freely flowed, yet not one act of unkindness have I heard reported as being committed by either regular or volunteer.

General Taylor, finding the field-pieces of little use, ordered us to retire to camp as soon as the volunteers had withdrawn.

Their withdrawal was ordered upon the supposition that General Worth would commence throwing shells into the city in the afternoon. The mortar was sent to him yesterday. It was a difficult matter to get the volunteers out; they were having their own fun. The enemy sent in a flag of truce today, asking a cessation until the women and children could be removed. The general, of course, declined; such a degree of politeness should not have been expected at this late hour. The flag is a good symptom; their time is drawing near. I hardly think they will hold out another day. It is reported many were leaving the heights with pack-mules this morning. Had not General Worth taken possession of the Saltillo road, I question whether many would not have been off yesterday. Thus far they have fought most bravely, and with an endurance and tenacity I did not think they possessed.

On our march back to camp, I was very much amused at a remark of an Irishman: "Faith, boys, we have had a Waterloo time of it; three days' fighting! The French fought against the combined powers of Europe; we are the combined powers of Europe and America! We have a little of all among us, and *the whole* can't be bate!"

. . . SEPTEMBER 24TH. In the morning all was quiet, and shortly after reveille we heard that Colonel Murino had arrived in camp with a flag of truce, and with an offer from General Ampudia to surrender the city, if General Taylor would permit him to march out with his troop and all the public property. General Taylor of course declined, and sent back his terms, stating an answer would be received at General Worth's headquarters at 12 M.; he repaired there immediately. Colonel Murino stated that they had received information that commissioners had been appointed to negotiate for peace, and that no re-enforcements would be sent them; that we *might* take the place, but that it would cost us two thirds of our command. It was understood, if terms were not agreed upon, firing would re-commence, and as night has arrived, I presume it is all settled.

If it is so, honorably, thanks be to God! I am tired of this spilling of blood.

SEPTEMBER 25TH. The general returned last night about 12 o'clock; the city has capitulated.

. . . The battle is over: the army, both regulars and volunteers — or, more properly speaking, Americans — have proved themselves invincible. Both officers and men, with death staring them in the face, did their duty without flinching, and with a bravery worthy of all praise.

* * *

SEPTEMBER 26TH. I rode to that city which has been the object of our hopes and fears since the 8th and 9th of May. On my way there, the first point of interest was the citadel, from which issued those spiteful cross-fires over the plain. It is a regular bastion-work, with revetments of solid masonry, having thirty-four embrasures. If the ditches had been dug out in front of the curtains, it could only have been taken by regular approaches. In its interior are the remains of an unfinished Cathedral, which of itself is a work of defense. Two magazines, filled with ammunition, were discovered, enough to have kept them shooting at us for a month.

The city is situated in a plain, open toward the south, and almost at the base of the Sierra Madre, whose towering peaks appear to overhang it. Directly north of the city, and between it and the mountains, flows the Arroyo Topa. Entering the city, I was immediately struck with the number of persons moving and getting ready to move. Every thing that bore the name of an animal was packed, and all appeared to be making their way out of the city as speedily as possible. In every street we passed works of defense, nearly all barricaded, the barricades lapping each other, and ditches in front of each. Every house was a fortification.

I rode to the Plaza, in which many of General Worth's division were comfortably quartered. The streets are well paved,

and the sidewalks have flat stones. In the center of the Plaza
there is a neat fountain; the houses are better built than any I
have yet seen; each one has its garden inclosed by high stone
walls, filled with oranges, pomegranates, grapes, and a profusion
of flowers. The quantities of beautiful trees scattered about
the city, the domes and minarets, give it a fairy-like aspect. A
great deal of fruit is exposed for sale in the Plaza; the grapes
are delicious. The market-men and women, with their quaint
dresses, are already on the move, and every thing betokens an
ample supply of vegetables.

Attracted by the sound of that everlasting *Mexican bugle*
(whose first notes were given to us at the Colorado), I discovered the Mexican troops were marching out. I saw many
of them pass. The infantry were miserably clad, brawny,
thick-set fellows, chiefly shod with sandals; one regiment of
Lancers were as fine looking men as I ever saw. Their horses
were inferior animals; *one* of ours could ride over *three* of
them. The streets were filled with the followers of the army,
mounted on every thing, from a decent mustang to an humble,
uncomplaining donkey. Some of the officers' wives, pictur-
esquely wrapped in their gay-colored ponchos, were slowly
riding after their chivalric husbands. The main Plaza is still
occupied by the enemy, to which we have no access. General
Ampudia left on the 25th, with two divisions of his army.

I visited Arista's Palace, which is directly under the hill on
which the Bishop's Palace is situated. It is a long, low, white
stone building, beautifully finished, claiming no particular order
of architecture, with flat roof, thick walls, and stone floors. At
the back of the house is a portico twenty feet in width, and a
garden that rivals Oriental magnificence. Double walls of
white masonry, about three feet high, filled in with earth, laid
out in fanciful figures, with fountains in the center, roses, and
numerous other plants, apparently growing out of the walls,
and also in the inclosed space; vases, with choice exotics, arranged round them; a bold stream of water, running through a
plaster raceway, leads to a marble bath, covered with trellis-

work, over which the grape and other vines clamber. In the
rear of this are beautiful groves of orange-trees and pomegranates, and a fine vegetable garden. Imagine the whole tastefully
laid out and kept in the neatest order, and you can form some
idea of one of the retreats of this Mexican nabob. It has been
turned into a hospital, in which the wounded of Worth's
division are lying. The oranges in the garden were kept for
the wounded; but immediately outside there was a wilderness
of them, where every one picked what they pleased. Some of
the houses occupied by the officers are very neatly, but simply
furnished; many of the walls are hung with mirrors and choice
paintings.

After riding over the city and examining minutely its defenses, my only astonishment is how they could yield it. It is
a perfect Gibraltar. At the eastern extremity, where so many
of our brave fellows fell, my wonder is that *any escaped*. There
is a system of batteries, the one defending the other. General
Worth conducted his movements with judgment and skill. His
motto on starting was, "*A grade or a grave.*" He escaped the
latter, and it is to be hoped he will obtain the former. . . .

CHAPTER 6   One of the
                        Greatest Blunders

Reaction to the American victory at Monterrey was mixed.
Newspapers in the United States praised Taylor and his men,
especially General Worth. But President Polk was dissatisfied.
He believed Taylor "had the enemy in his power and should
have taken them prisoners . . . and preserved the advantage
which he had obtained by pushing on without further delay
into the country. . . ." Some officers also believed Taylor had
made some serious tactical mistakes. He had overestimated the
destructive force of his own artillery and underestimated the
strength of the Mexican works. Moreover, he had dispersed
his attack. One of the officers critical of Taylor's generalship
at Monterrey was Captain Benjamin Franklin Cheatham (1820–
1886), a Tennessee volunteer.

CAPTAIN   BENJAMIN   FRANKLIN   CHEATHAM
Two Letters to his Sisters, October 6 and 16, 1846
Benjamin Franklin Cheatham Papers,
Tennessee State Library and Archives, Nashville

October 6, 1846
. . . I visited the Cathedral which is a very large, and I may
say the finest building that I have ever seen in Mexico. It was
the headquarters of Ampudia during the battle, and had a very

large supply of ammunition of all kinds in it. On the third day, Capt Ridgley who belongs to the Artillery, and who was stationed with us in the fort that we took on the first day, spent most of his time in shooting at the Cathedral with a nine pounder that we took in the fort, with their own ammunition. I afterwards saw that he hit it four times but on ac[coun]t of the distance, did but little damage; he is a splendid officer, and the bravest and most reckless man, that I ever saw. In this engagement, the artillerymen, or cavalry, neither had an opportunity of doing much, because the artillery we had was too light to damage the strong walls. I consider that old Taylor committed one of the greatest blunders that ever a General was guilty of in coming here to attack one of the strongest fortified towns in Mexico, with nothing in the world but small artillery for open field fighting; the same that was used upon the open prairies on the 8th & 9th and when we were drawn up before the strong walls and batteries of Monterey, we had but one alternative, which was to charge upon their strongly mounted forts, strongly supported with their infantry, and drive them from their guns at point of bayonett, which I am proud to say Old Tennessee did gallant style. We took into the field three hundred and forty men, and had killed and wounded one hundred and four. So you see that we had killed and wounded near[l]y one third of our force, which is a thing almost unheard of. The Mexicans say that we are the first people that they ever saw run up into the cannon's mouth, they wanted to know where we came from, and what kind of people we were. . . .

*   *   *

October 16, 1846

. . . The health of our Regiment has been worse than any other in the service, in fact it has been the unlucky Regiment of the Army from the commencement. It not only suffered from sickness and disease, but we had the misfortune when brought into battle to suffer more than any other two Regiments. Although we only carried into action three hundred and forty men we lost twenty seven killed and seventy seven wounded, in all one hundred and four, since then six of the wounded have died. . . .

There has been an attempt made by the Mississippians to claim the honor of having been first in the fort, that was taken by our Brigade on 21st. It is the most rascally, ungentlemanly, and unsoldier like piece of conduct that was ever heard of to undertake to rob us of the honour and glory that we had won, at the cost of so many of Tennessee's noble sons. Here throughout the army it is not doubted, and we have the *honour* of having been first in the fort, after one of the most desperate charges ever heard of. I must here say, that I consider that our division of the army was badly managed, that we were rushed headlong into the fight, even our Generals did not know where we were going and what our situation was until we found ourselves under a deadly cross fire of cannon balls, shells, grape and musketry, from three different forts, without any chance of extricating ourselves except by charging at the mouth of the cannon, the forts in our front.

CHAPTER 7

My Proposed Theatre Is Different

Before Taylor could undertake another campaign, he learned that he was no longer the principal American commander in Mexico. His actions, especially the armistice he had granted the Mexicans after the fall of Monterrey, had displeased President Polk, who wrote in his diary on November 14: "The Cabinet fully discussed the conduct of General Taylor and were agreed that he was unfit for the chief command, that he had not mind enough for the station, that he was a bitter political partisan, and had no sympathies with the administration." The President ordered Winfield Scott (1786–1866), the army's senior general, to Mexico to supersede Taylor. For a time Scott, called "Fuss and Feathers" for his dress and decorum, had supported Taylor's operations, but after the Battle of Monterrey he had changed his mind and persuaded the administration to let him land an American army at Vera Cruz and move westward toward Mexico City.

In a letter to Taylor, Scott explained part of his plan.

GENERAL WINFIELD SCOTT
Letter to General Zachary Taylor, November 25, 1846
Zachary Taylor Papers, Library of Congress, Washington, D.C.

Nov. 25, 1846

MY DEAR GENERAL:

I left Washington late in the day yesterday, and expect to embark for New Orleans the 30th instant. By the 12th of December I may be in that city, at Point Isabel the 17th, and Camargo, say the 23rd — in order to be within easy corresponding distance from you. It is not probable that I may be able to visit Monterey, and circumstances may prevent your coming to me. I shall much regret not having an early opportunity of felicitating you in person upon your many brilliant achievements; but we may meet somewhere in the interior of Mexico.

I am not coming, my dear General, to supersede you in the immediate command on the line of operations rendered illustrious by you and your gallant army. My proposed theatre is different. You may imagine it, and I wish very much that it were prudent, at this distance, to tell you all that I expect to attempt or hope, to execute. I have been admonished that despatches have been lost, and I have no special messages at hand. Your imagination will be aided by the letters of the Secretary of War, conveyed by Mr. Armistead, Major Graham and Mr. McLane.

But, my dear General, I shall be obliged to take from you most of the gallant officers and men (regular & volunteers) whom you have so long and so nobly commanded. I am afraid that I shall, by imperious necessity — the approach of yellow fever on the gulf coast — reduce you, for a time, to stand on the defensive. This will be infinitely painful to you, and for that reason distressing to me. But I rely upon your patriotism to submit to the temporary sacrifice with cheerfulness. No man can better afford to do so. Recent victories place you on that high eminence, and I even flatter myself that any benefit that may result to me personally, from the unequal division of troops alluded to, will lessen the pain of your consequent inactivity.

You will be aware of the recent call for nine regiments of new volunteers, including one of Texas horse. The President may soon ask for many more, and we are not without hope that Congress may add ten or twelve to the regular establishment. These by the spring, say April, may by the aid of large bounties, be in the field — should Mexico not earlier propose terms of accommodation, and long before the spring, (March) it is probable you will be again in force to resume offensive operations.

I am writing at a late hour of the night and more than half sick of a cold. I may dispatch another note before I embark, but, from New Orleans, Point Isabel, &c., you shall hear from me officially and fully.

It was not possible for me to find time to write from Washington, as I much desired. I only received an intimation to hold myself in preparation for Mexico, on the 18th instant. Much has been done toward that end, and more remains to be executed.

Your detailed report of the operations of Monterey, and reply to the Secretary's despatch, by Lieutenant [Lewis A.] Armistead, were both received two days after I was instructed to proceed south.

In haste, my dear General,

I remain, Yours faithfully.

WINFIELD SCOTT

CHAPTER 8   I Truly Fear
Their Plans

Scott's letter incensed Taylor. He sent official protests to Scott, Secretary of War Marcy, and President Polk. It would be better to relieve him, Taylor suggested, than to deprive him of his experienced soldiers. Why had the government failed to inform him earlier of plans to weaken his army? "I am constrained to believe that I no longer possess the confidence of the administration," Taylor wrote. And in much less restrained letters to his brother, Taylor revealed his resentment and suspicion.

GENERAL   ZACHARY   TAYLOR
Two Letters to Colonel Joseph P. Taylor,
January 14, February 8, 1847
Zachary Taylor Papers, Library of Congress, Washington, D.C.

(Private)
Janry, 14th 1847
MY DEAR JOSEPH,

Your very kind & interesting letter of Janry, inst. this moment reached me with despatches from Major Genl. Scott, of most extraordinary character; the course which [he] is now pursuing cannot be misunderstood, it is to break me down, a plan concocted by Scott, [Secretary of War William L.] Marcy & Worth; which was to strip me of my command or the greater part of those that could be relied on, under the expectation that I would either leave the country in disgust, or be driven from it by the enemy, in either case they & their creatures would make the most of it; & I can only say I truly fear their plans have been too well concocted to be avoided; but I will try to act with great prudence & do all I can to avoid the coils which have been spread for me, & yet hope that some of those poor & contemptible creatures will be entangled in the snares they have spread for others. Had Genl S. been sent out with orders to supersede me, & left it optional for me to have retired or served under his, Genl Scott's orders, I should have thought nothing of it, but would have turned over the command or laid it down with much more pleasure than I ever assumed it; as in that case no responsibility would have rested on my shoulders, but this would not have answered their malignant ends; the people would have asked why this was done, or why I was relieved or suspended; which they would not liked to have answered; they therefore determined the safest way was to place me in a position that let me act as I would. I could not short of a miracle prevent subjecting myself or laying myself liable to censure which is the position they wished to place me in.

. . . I shall leave here [Victoria] tomorrow or early the next day & trace my steps to Monterey, & if I can do so with propriety will leave the country soon after reaching there; but this I will not do without due consideration, or in a way which will give my enemies an advantage over me, which I am satisfied they greatly desire I would do.

P.S.
I write in great haste & by candle light having only a few moments or a very short time to do so as I wish the express to leave early tomorrow morning.

Z. T.

*   *   *

February 8, 1847

. . . As to Genl. Scott's professions I hold them in great contempt, acts are stronger than professions; I am perfectly
satisfied that he has been a prominent participator with a party
if not the principal one, to outrage me as far as he or they
could go.

. . . I believe they [Taylor's troops] are ready to meet the
enemy at any moment, no matter as to numbers. . . . I shall in a
day or two have near 5,000 men, . . . the greater portion of
them will be volunteers yet I have no fears but we will give
a satisfactory account of the enemy, should he have the temer-
ity to attack us. In a communication I have just received from
Genl. Scott in reply to one I wrote him from Victoria, no
means of a conciliatory character, he advises me to fall back
on Monterey; in reply to the same I have informed him I would
do no such thing without orders to that effect from proper
authority.

CHAPTER *9*   The Best Reply

In February 1847 Zachary Taylor left Monterrey in defiance of orders to remain inactive and on the defensive. When he met General Antonio Lopez de Santa Anna and 20,000 Mexican soldiers south of Saltillo, Taylor posted his 4,800 men in a defensive position near Buena Vista Ranch. Santa Anna, convinced that he had an overwhelming advantage, demanded unconditional surrender. Taylor refused, and on February 22 his infantry and artillery repulsed several determined Mexican assaults on the left and center of the American position. That night Santa Anna withdrew from the field and returned to Mexico City. Thus ended the war in northern Mexico. The Americans settled into the routine of an occupation army.

In a letter to his brother, Taylor explained why he fought at Buena Vista.

GENERAL ZACHARY TAYLOR
Letter to Colonel Joseph P. Taylor, March 27, 1847
Zachary Taylor Papers, Library of Congress, Washington, D.C.

March 27, 1847

MY DEAR COL,

Your highly esteemed & interesting letters of the 12th ulto. reached me about the first inst. the information in relation to the intentions & movements of the enemy as communicated to you by the individual referred to in Matamoros was no doubt entirely correct, but reached me too late to have benefited by the same, even had it been in my power to have taken advantage of it. I wrote you immediately after the battle of Buena Vista by Major Coffee of the pay dept., informing you of the repulse of the enemy, in addition to the loss of some of your particular friends but all communication having been cut off between this & the Rio Grande for some time, you would not have recd. my letter for a considerable time after it was written. The enemy after continuing the fight with great energy throughout the entire day of the 23rd fell back to Agua Nueva 12 miles during the night, without our knowledge leaving his killed & many of his wounded, for us to bury & take care of, we lying on our arms all night, without fires, there being no wood in the country, with the mercury considerably below the freezing point, ready & expecting to renew the contest in the morning but on reconnoitering their position at day light, found they had retreated and did not think it advisable to pursue, not knowing whether they would renew the attack, continue the retreat, or wished to draw us from our strong position, we therefore contented ourselves with closely watching his movements until the 26th, when finding they had recommenced their retreat, the army was put in march for Agua Nueva where he had halted, early on the morning of the 27th, & reached their place of encampment on the same evening, his rear guard consisting of lancers, leaving as our advance got in sight; I determined on pursuing & harassing his rear, but on examining the state of the men & horses found that five days marching, incessant watching in addition to 16 hours hard fighting had so exhausted the first & broken the latter that it was next to impossible to accomplish anything of importance without rest & abandoned my intention, remaining quiet until the 2d inst. when I pushed a command forward on the San Luis Potosi road the one on which they advanced & retreated 25 miles to Encarnacion a large ranch where Major [John P.]

Gaines & party were captured; & where the Mier prisoners were decimated & every tenth man shot, the first water on said route where was found between two & three hundred wounded Mexicans with between fifty & sixty soldiers to take care of them, in the most wretched condition, so much so that I authorised Captain Eaton of your dept. to send them some supplies to prevent their starving, from the public stores which if not approved of at Washington, I will cheerfully pay for; the great loss on both sides particularly on ours of persons of so much worth, intelligence & patriotism, amazed even some of my warm personal friends, that it has deprived me of everything like pleasure or gratification when I reflect at the cost the victory in question was won; & when I consider too the outrageous manner I was stripped of nearly all the regular troops, & more than one half the volunteers & left on to defend a line of near four hundred miles in extent & to keep up several garrisons for the protection of large depots with about 800 regulars & between 6 & 7 thousand volunteers in front of & in striking distance of a well organized & appointed army of Mexicans of 30,000; the largest force which I could possibly bring together to oppose which was rather less than 500 regulars, a portion of them recruits, & not exceeding 4,000 volunteers who could be brought into battle; yet with this small force after a most sanguinary fight with the sanction of divine providence, we succeeded in repulsing the immense disparity of force opposed to us, & compelled them to return who survived the contest from whence they came, will as no doubt disappoint Marcy, Scott & Co., who had calculated on different results. Had they left me 1,000, or even 500 regulars I feel the Mexican Army would have been completely broken down the whole of his artillery, & baggage captured or destroyed; why I was left with so inadequate a force is a mystery which Marcy & Scott alone can solve, & which I hope the next Congress will compel them to do, & that the people will drive the former from the position he has so eminently disguised — I cannot but entertain the opinion that the worthies referred to racked their brains much

more to break me down than they did Santa Anna, & as they
thought that as public opinion might not altogether like such
a course it was thought most advisable to strip me of the greater
portion of my command, under the expectation that it would
drive me from the country, or if I remained & the enemy
driven to or beyond the Rio Grande, in either case my reputation as a military man would have been blighted, but matters
have so turned out as greatly to disappoint them; & I have the
gratification of knowing without one particle of vanity entering
into the matter, that by pursuing the course I did, I have saved
the honor of our country & our glorious flag from being trailed
in the dust; for had I left for the U. States on the receipt of
Genl. Scott's most unmilitary as well as outrageous order,
leaving me as he supposed at the mercy of the enemy, I hazard
nothing in saying we would not now have held a single post
on this side of the Rio Grande except on the sea coast, other
than Matamoros & Monterey, the latter of which would now
have been closely besieged, & must have surrendered had Genl.
Scott not at once released his ships with his army, & opened
the communications between it & the Rio Grande which would
have been entirely cut off & could only have been restored by
his doing so. I was advised by Genl. Scott as well as Genl.
Butler to fall back from Saltillo & concentrate my forces on
Monterey, had I done so the most disastrous consequences
would have grown out of it.

The attacks made upon me in the House of Representatives
. . . & in the Senate . . . was doubtless all done by order, which
however gives me but little concern, & it seems to me the battle
of Buena Vista is the best reply I can make to their contemptible attacks; the fact is I have been constantly but under-
standably assailed by the dept, ever since the battle of Monterey
nor have a single communication addressed by me to the department for the last five months been replied to, or the receipt
even acknowledged.

What effect the battle of Buena Vista will have on Genl.
Santa Anna, the Mexican congress, as well as a majority of their

people in the way of opening negotiations for peace time must
determine, but I hope it will have the most favorable results
in that way. The effect my official report of said battle will
have on the Secretary of War, so far as to teach him some of
the courtesies of a gentleman, in which he is greatly deficient,
so far as replying to or acknowledging its receipt, time must
also determine; but even if he neglects to do so, I think public
opinion will compel him to say or give my dispatch to the
country through the public journals; as the Secy. has recently
read me a pretty rough lecture on the impropriety of writing
a private letter to Genl. Gaines in November last, which found
its way into the newspapers. This he would hardly have ven-
tured to have done to the extent he did, had he not supposed
that he & Scott had left me powerless, in pursuing the course
they had towards me, but in this he has become satisfied he
fired before he was ready, & would gladly recall his dirty
epistle if he could; in reply I informed him that the letter in
question was never intended for the press of which there was
sufficient evidence on its face, nor would I have authorized its
publication under any circumstances, had I been consulted in
regard to the matter but as it had been done I cared nothing
about it, that on reading it over much more carefully than I
had done I saw nothing improper or objectionable in it; that
it was not intended to assail any one much less the administration or any member of it; nor did I see when & how it had
done so, that after the most mature reflection I would not alter
a line or word in it & that I asked no favors nor shrank from
any responsibility; I concluded by referring him to one of
Aesop's fables from which he may draw the moral.

   . . . I left Saltillo about the 8th of the present month &
reached here the next day & found matters & things rather in a
bad way between this & the Rio Grande, the enemy having
cut off our communications between this & that river, & being
then in possession of the country; having taken & destroyed
some 160 wagons & teams with their loads but with the exception of a few robbers who may continue to infest the

country, I think the regular cavalry of the enemy will soon if they have not already retired beyond the Sierra Madre.

We have this moment recd. a copy of an address of Genl. S[cott] addressed to his army dated at San Luis Potosi, the 14th ins. in which he says he was about to take up his line of march for the City of Mexico, in order to take matters entirely into his own hands, to put down civil dissensions, discords &c. &c. as there had been much fighting there on the 6th, 7th, & 8th, ins. so that we hardly need expect him in this quarter at any rate for some time to come.

If you can do so without inconvenience, I would be glad if you would purchase me four first rate mules of the country, if they can be had, gentle ones, at Matamoros & have them shipped to N. Orleans to the care of M. White & Co., to be sent by them on their arrival, to the plantation. But unless it can be done without putting you to inconvenience do not attempt it.

If there are any old whisky at the Brazos in the commissaries dept. send me a barrel for head quarters to Camargo with directions for it to be forwarded here by the first train.

I am very anxious to hear from Washington up to the close of last session, to see what was finally done in regard to bringing about a peace, or to carry on the war with vigor, all of which information you must have at Matamoros by this time.

I understand that [Lewis] Cass in a speech in the Senate in relation to the war quoted from a letter recd. from [General Thomas S.] Jesup in relation to transportation, as an indirect attack on me, to discredit my statement in regard to the same done no doubt by order; the statement of J. was made without the slightest foundation so far as truth was concerned; but I pity rather than censure him for the same, for poor man, I have not considered him entirely sane since he wrote that unfortunate Blair letter; & it is very unkind in such men as Cass to expose his unfortunate situation by quoting from his letters & parading his erroneous statements before the country.

CHAPTER 10   Victory Without Parallel

Most of the Americans who fought at Buena Vista were in-experienced volunteers; only 700 of Taylor's 4,800 men had ever seen combat before. Some of these volunteers broke ranks and ran during the battle. Others fought bravely against tre-mendous odds. Brigadier General Joseph Lane, called by a regular army officer "the prince of loafers & blackguards," commanded the Third Brigade of Indiana Volunteers at Buena Vista. In his official report of the battle, Lane defended him-self and his men.

BRIGADIER GENERAL JOSEPH LANE
Official Report of the Battle of Buena Vista
Senate Executive Documents, No. 1, 30 Cong.,
1 Sess., Vol. 1, pp. 181–184

Feb. 25, 1847

SIR

I have the honor of laying before you the following report of that part of the battle of the 22d and 23d inst., in which the forces under my immediate command took part.

In obedience to your orders on the 22d, I took position on the left of the field upon which the battle was fought, near the foot of the mountain, with the eight battalion companies of the 2d regiment of my brigade, supported by three pieces of light artillery, commanded by Lieutenant [John Paul Jones] O'Brien. The four rifle companies of this brigade (two from the 2d, and two from the 3d regiments) having been sent, under your orders, together with two companies of Kentucky mounted riflemen, to occupy an eminence and ridge on the side of the mountain, to check the advance of the enemy (two regiments) who were attempting to turn the left flank of my position by climbing the sides of the mountain.

Those rifle companies took their position in the afternoon of the 22d — the four companies of Indiana, commanded by Major [Willis A.] Gorman, of the 3d regiment — the whole under the command of Colonel [Humphrey] Marshall, of Kentucky; and soon afterwards the enemy opened a brisk fire upon our forces, but with little effect, which they continued without intermission for three hours. In the mean time, my men, being secure from the enemy's balls, and watching their chances, and taking good aim, succeeded in killing and wounding some thirty or forty of the enemy. In this engagement my loss was four men slightly wounded.

During the night of the 22d the enemy sent a reinforcement of about 1,600 men up the mountain, and succeeded in occupying heights which commanded the position of the riflemen. My whole command slept upon the field that night on their arms. As soon as it was light, on the morning of the 23d, the enemy opened a severe fire from their whole force on the mountain, now amounting in all to about 2,500 or 3,000 men, commanded by the Mexican Colonel Ampudia, it is believed. Notwithstanding the great superiority of the enemy in numbers, our gallant riflemen held them in check for several hours, killing and wounding some fifty or sixty of their forces.

About 8 o'clock, A.M., of the 23d, I sent a part of the Kentucky mounted riflemen and cavalry, (dismounted for that purpose) up the side of the mountain to support the forces already there, at which time the fire of the enemy became tremendous, but which was returned by our gallant force for more than one hour longer. My instructions from yourself were to hold my position on the left of the field against any force which the enemy might bring against me in that quarter. The enemy had been in great force all the morning of the 23d, directly in my front, and in my sight, but too far distant to be reached by Lieut. O'Brien's battery.

About 9 o'clock I was informed by Colonel Churchill that the enemy were advancing towards my position in great force, sheltering themselves in a deep ravine which runs up towards the mountain directly in my front. I immediately put my columns in motion, consisting of those eight battalion companies and Lieut. O'Brien's battery, amounting in all to about 400 men, to meet them. The enemy, when they deployed from the ravine, and appeared on the ridge, displayed a force of about 4,000 infantry, supported by a large body of lancers. The infantry immediately opened a most destructive fire, which was returned by my small command, both infantry and artillery, in a most gallant manner for some time. I soon perceived that I was too far from the enemy for my muskets to take that deadly effect which I desired, and immediately sent my aid-de-camp to Lieut. O'Brien, directing him to place his battery in a more advanced position, with the determination of advancing my whole line. By this movement I should not only be near the enemy, but should also bring the company on my extreme left more completely into action, as the brow of the hill impeded their fire. By this time the enemy's fire of musketry and the raking fire of ball and grape shot of their battery posted on my left flank had become terrible, and my infantry instead of advancing, as was ordered, I regret to say retired in some disorder from their position, notwithstanding my own and the severe efforts of my officers to prevent them. About the same time, the riflemen and cavalry on the mountain retired to the plain below. The Arkansas cavalry (who had been posted by your orders in my rear at the foot of the mountain to act as circumstances might require) also left their position, the whole making a retrograde movement along the plain towards the rear. At the same time one of the Illinois regiments, not under my command, but stationed at some distance in rear and on the right of my position, also retired to the rear. These troops, the most of them, were immediately rallied, and fought during the whole day like veterans. A few of them, I regret to say did not return to the field at all. By this apparent success the enemy were much elated, and poured down along the side of the mountain on the extreme left of the field their thousands of infantry and lancers, and formed themselves in good order along the mountain fronting perpendicularly to where our lines had been posted. At this critical juncture, the Mississippi regiment, under the command of Colonel [Jefferson] Davis, arrived on the field, and being joined by a part of the 2d Indiana, met the enemy in a most gallant style, and, after a severe and bloody engagement, repulsed them with great loss. In the mean time a large body of lancers, 600 to 800 in number, who had passed down along the left towards our rear, made a most desperate charge upon the Arkansas and Kentucky cavalry, with a view of cutting off and plundering the baggage train of the army which was at a *ranche* near the battle-field.

This charge was met and resisted most gallantly by those cavalry, aided by about 200 infantry, who had taken refuge there after they had retired from the field. This repulse discouraged the enemy, and the Mississippi regiment, and part of the 2d Indiana, being joined by the 3d Indiana regiment, commanded by Colonel James H. Lane, now advanced up towards the foot of the mountain for the purpose of dislodging the enemy's force stationed there. In this enterprise I was aided by Captain ——'s battery, of light artillery, and it was crowned with complete success; the enemy retreating in disorder, and with immense loss, back along the side of the mountain to the position which they had occupied in the morning; some flying in terror up the sides of the mountain, and into the ravines, while a few were taken prisoners. Amongst the last desperate attempts of the enemy to regain and hold the left of the field, was a charge made by a large body of lancers upon my command. This charge, for gallantry and determined bravery on both sides, has been seldom equalled. The forces on either side were nearly equal in numbers. Instead of throwing my command into squares to resist the charge, the enemy were received in line of two ranks, my force reserving its fire until the enemy were within about seventy yards, which was delivered with a deadly aim, and which proved most destructive in its effects — the enemy flying in every direction in disorder, and making a precipitate retreat towards their own lines. About sunset the enemy withdrew from the field, and the battle ceased. In a brief report it is impossible to enter into the details of a day like the 23d. The fighting throughout consisted of different engagements in different parts of the field, the whole of them warm and well contested; many of them bloody and terrible. The men under my command actually discharged eighty and some ninety rounds of cartridges at the enemy during the day. The 2d regiment of my command which opened the battle on the plain, in such gallant style, deserves a passing remark. I shall attempt to make no apology for their retreat; for it was their duty to stand or die to the last man until they received orders to retire; but I desire to call your attention to one fact connected with this affair. They remained in their position, in line, receiving the fire of 3,000 or 4,000 infantry in front, exposed at the same time on the left flank to a most desperate raking fire from the enemy's battery, posted within point-blank shot, until they had deliberately discharged *twenty rounds* of cartridges at the enemy.

Some excuse may be framed for those who retired for a few minutes and then immediately rallied, and fought during the day; but unless they hasten to retrieve their reputations, disgrace must forever hang about the names of those who refused to return, and I regret to say there were a few of those from nearly every volunteer corps engaged.

In a battle so fierce and protracted as this, where there were so many exhibitions of coolness and bravery, it is a difficult and delicate task to particularize. But justice compels me to mention Colonel Davis and his regiment of Mississippians, who so nobly and so bravely came to the rescue at the proper time to save the fortunes of the day.

Colonel J. H. Lane and the 3d regiment of my command were ordered into the action soon after Colonel Davis; and the coolness and bravery displayed by both the officers and men of that regiment have rarely been equalled — never surpassed — by any troops, at any time. They have done infinite honor to the State and nation that gave them birth. Lieutenant Colonel Hadden, of the regiment of my brigade, aided me in rallying his regiment after they retired; and he in person succeeded in marching a party of them back towards the enemy, with whom he immediately became engaged, and fortunately repulsed them with considerable loss. In another part of the field he succeeded in killing an officer of the enemy with his own hand, by sending a rifle ball through him at a great distance.

I was also much indebted to Major Mooney, quartermaster; Major Dix, paymaster; the gallant and lamented Captain Lincoln, of General Wool's staff; and to Lieutenant Robinson, for their assistance in rallying the forces after they had retired from their position. They all behaved nobly, and deserve the thanks of the country for the coolness and intrepidity which they displayed on that trying occasion. The latter, acting as my aid-de-camp during the entire day, is entitled to particular attention for the gallant manner in which he executed my orders. Lieutenant O'Brien, who commanded the battery of light artillery on my right, is deserving of particular praise for his courage and self-possession throughout the day, moving and discharging his battery with all the coolness and precision of a day of ordinary parade. Major Mooney, quartermaster, and Major Morrison, commissary, attached to my brigade, although not belonging to the line of the army, nor expected to take an active part in the battle, are entitled to great honor for their bravery and coolness in promptly rallying the scattered forces at the ranche, who assisted, under the command of Major Morrison, in resisting the desperate charge of the lancers made upon the Arkansas and Kentucky cavalry, as, by this repulse, the whole baggage train of the army was saved from destruction. This important duty they discharged, in addition to those which strictly appertained to their respective departments. A statement of the killed and wounded has already been submitted, which need not be recapitulated here. Although censure does justly attach to a few who proved recreant to their duty on that day, yet I am of the opinion that veteran troops, either of this or any other country, could not have fought and won the battle better than those engaged. It is a victory without a parallel in this or any other war on this continent; and the men and officers who did their duty at the battle of Buena Vista deserve to have their names inscribed on the brightest pages of their country's history.

CHAPTER 11

In Shameful
Confusion

One of the most outspoken critics of volunteers was Captain
Braxton Bragg (1817–1876) of North Carolina, a West Pointer
and battery commander who later became a Confederate general. He had been with Taylor's army from the time it landed
at Corpus Christi, and had received brevet promotions for gallant conduct at Fort Brown, Monterrey, and Buena Vista,
where his guns helped check several Mexican assaults. In a letter to his friend Lieutenant William T. Sherman, Bragg denounced the actions of volunteer units at Buena Vista.

CAPTAIN BRAXTON BRAGG
Letter to William T. Sherman, March 1, 1848
William T. Sherman Papers, Library of Congress, Washington, D.C.

March 1, 1848

For the details of the military operations &c on this line I refer
you to Genl Taylor's despatches. They are generously full so
far as good conduct went, but rather silent on the subject of
volunteers running &c &c. A few facts on this subject may
interest you. The great Baltimore Battalion which boasted so
much of taking Monterey fled in a body very early in the
action and never got into the fight. From five companies but

nine men remained on the field at night. With the exception
of the Miss. regt. under Col. Davis, a graduate [of the United
States Military Academy], you may say *ditto* of almost all who
were here. The extolled Texans in every instance were not
sustained and urged on by regular troops have retreated —
frequently in shameful confusion — from equal or inferior
numbers — but when the plundering, murdering & ravishing
commenced — like Sam Reed's "John Donkey" — you might
always put them down for "two chances." At the Battle of
Buena Vista we were whipped, and in retreat when Genl. Taylor, about 9 A.M. arrived on the ground with the Miss. Reg^t,
2d. Drag. and Kilburns gun of my battery. Three regt — 2d.
Ind., Ky. & Ark's Horse, and parts of some others — were in
full retreat — but few of these ever returned to the field, and
when the day closed we could not have mustered 2500 men. It
is a fact, asserted by our Medical Officer, that the wounded in
the hospitals were trampled to death by refugees endeavoring
to hide and pass for sick or wounded. And yet, that was a
volunteer victory!! If any action in the whole war, Cump,
proved the inefficiency of Vols. that is the one. With any one
of our old regular Inf[antr]y regts. we would have carried
the enemy's art[iller]y and destroyed his army. This all the
Vols. at first acknowledged & did not presume on claiming
credit until the papers from home put the idea into their heads,
and now they really *believe* that *they* gained the day. With the
exceptions above they did well — very well for Volunteers —
and that's all you can say. Nothing under Heaven would have
saved us there but the *prestige* of old Zack. Wool advised a
retreat and had Washington's battery on the move (the caissons) when Don Z. interfered and saved us. This is all denied
now with solemnity and indignation, but still its true. Old Z.
has said so, and officers who heard the order still repeat it —
among them Henry Whiting 4th Arty. Indeed, Cump, to go to
the merits of the case, no man after the valiant Lt. Col. M[ay]
2d drag[oon]s deserved so little credit at Buena Vista as Genl
Wool. He is now our Comd'g Genl and the weakest and most

contemptible apology for a great man I have had the misfortune to meet. He is equally as weak a man as [Colonel
William] Gates, with a little more education which has only
seemed to increase his dishonesty. It would require a volume
to detail his many little dirty acts. But one as a sample. He
sustains from the revenues of the city a dirty, filthy little 4 x 5
newspaper in Monterey, printed by soldiers on extra duty,
devoted solely and entirely to puffing "Gen¹ Wool — the real
Hero of Buena Vista," and his bedfellow the political Co¹ of
the 16. Inf J. W. Tibbatts — By the bye — these new reg^{ts} are
more than volunteers & proved themselves so at Mexico. They
have the finest material in the world but their officers are
mostly unfit for the service. See the great number run out of
service, many for bad conduct before the enemy. I pray to
God & hope, with some reason too, that the war may last till
Mr Polk goes out of office. For the Lord save us if he reduces
the army.

PART TWO

*With Scott from Vera Cruz
to Mexico City*

CHAPTER 12   Havoc and
                              Destruction

Private George Ballentine, who had previously served in the
British army, wrote what is perhaps the best account of Scott's
campaign by either an enlisted man or an officer. Unable to
find work as a weaver in America after he migrated from Scotland, Ballentine enlisted in the United States Army for five
years, and in February 1847 he was sent to join Scott's expedition. Ballentine described the capture of Vera Cruz in his
autobiography.

PRIVATE   GEORGE   BALLENTINE
Autobiography of an English Soldier in the United States Army
New York, Stringer & Townsend, 1853, pp. 141–166

. . . Our troops, a large proportion of whom were raw
recruits, were kept closely at drill while we lay in camp at
Tampico, and by the end of February they were considered in
good order for active operations. General Scott's arrival about
the 20th was a signal to be ready for a move, and in a day or
two after, the army received orders to embark; the first of the
troops going on board on the 24th.

Several days were occupied in getting all the men and horses
on board, but on the 27th of February all were ready to sail.

The regiment to which I belonged, being in the last division, had no delay; and getting into a steamer at the wharf at Tampico, we were taken down the river and put on board the barque *Caroline*, with all our baggage, in a few hours. We were no sooner on board than we began to weigh anchor, and in a very short time all our transports had spread their canvas to the breeze. Our fleet, comprising nearly a hundred sailing vessels, fifty or sixty of which were large ships and the remainder brigs and schooners, presented a very imposing appearance during the afternoon. The change of position perpetually occurring in the different vessels, caused by the difference in their rates of sailing, created excitement among the men, and added variety and animation to the scene. The number of large ships filled with troops, stores, and ammunition, and the strength of our whole armament, as compared with anything which Mexico could furnish, inspired our men with the certainty of success in the reduction of Vera Cruz. As to the cost of life involved in the undertaking, that was left to the chapter of accidents; in reckoning the probable contingencies of a coming engagement, the soldier seldom includes himself in the list of the killed and wounded. Our destination for the time was the island of Lobos, that being the place appointed for the whole vessels belonging to the expedition to rendezvous, preparatory to sailing for the harbour of Vera Cruz. We had a smart gale of wind during the night, and next morning we could only discern two or three vessels in the horizon out of the large fleet which had sailed with us on the previous day. We arrived at Lobos about five o'clock of the same evening, and came to anchor; having beaten every vessel of the expedition. The others continued to drop in by twos and threes until the middle of the day, by which time they had all come to anchor.

Lobos is a small sandy island not far from the coast, between Tampico and Vera Cruz. It is not seen until the voyager is close upon it, as it is very little above the level of the sea.

While we lay there, as there was a slight gale of wind, the sea broke in a heavy surf on the barren and desolate spot, on which the only signs of vegetation were a few stunted shrubs, evidently struggling hard with the difficulties of their situation for a bare subsistence. Three or four vessels from New Orleans were lying here on our arrival; they formed part of the expedition, and were waiting for us; a few of their passengers had gone ashore and pitched tents, preferring to sleep on the solid sand to the pitching of the vessel. All our fleet having arrived, on the morning of the 1st March we again set sail for Vera Cruz, which we reached on the evening of the 2nd, and came to anchor about eight miles from the castle of San Juan de Ulloa, the name of the fortification at Vera Cruz, about four miles from Sacrificios, a small island near the castle, where "men-of-war" anchor.

On the morning of the third, General Scott summoned the city and castle of Vera Cruz to surrender; and after a delay of several days, consumed in discussion by the military governor and the civil authorities, the latter of whom were in favour of a surrender, a definitive answer was returned to General Scott that he might come and take them if he could. San Juan is a very strong fortification built upon a small island in the bay, about three quarters of a mile from the pier at Vera Cruz. It had a garrison of between five and six thousand men, was well supplied with ammunition, and bristling with cannon, of which it had about a hundred, some of them of very heavy calibre. The buildings in the castle are all bombproof, and with the sea wall, are built of a soft species of coral, in which cannon balls are imbedded without producing the usual shattering and crumbling effect of these missiles on stone of a harder quality, and which is necessary to cause a breach. It was generally considered impregnable, and could only be approached by vessels on one side, a coral reef stretching round it on every side except the one facing the town. The city of Vera Cruz is surrounded with a wall about twelve or fifteen feet high, but which could be easily breached, and there are a number of half moon batteries round it well manned with guns; it is about three miles in circumference.

Having received the answer of the governor refusing to surrender, on the evening of the 7th General Scott issued an order for the troops to prepare for landing next morning. Commanding officers were directed to see their men furnished with two days' provisions in their havresacks, and that they had their canteens slung, and filled with water. Each man was also to take either his great-coat or his blanket with him, leaving the remainder of his clothes and necessaries, packed in his knapsack, on board. On the morning of the 8th, however, a stiff breeze having commenced to blow, the surf was too heavy for landing, and the order was countermanded. On the evening of the 8th the order of the previous evening was re-issued for the next morning, which having turned out fine, shortly after sunrise we began to get into the boats.

* * *

The surf-boats used for our disembarkation, had been expressly made for the purpose, for which they were admirably adapted, being strong, light, and roomy, and carrying about a hundred men with ease. The whole of the troops had been told off into three divisions, which had to be transferred from the vessels they were in, to those denominated in the order. When all were ready, at a signal from the vessel in which General Scott was, we were to get under weigh for Sacrificios, where we were to drop anchor and disembark at a distance of four miles from the city of Vera Cruz. The regiment to which I belonged was transferred to the deck of the Porpoise man-of-war brig. Between ten and eleven o'clock A.M., the troops having been all arranged on the vessels, on board of which they had been ordered to proceed, we got under weigh; but as the breeze was against us we had to beat up, and a number of the vessels were towed up by steamers. It was nearly four o'clock before we had all dropped anchor at Sacrificios.

Of vessels of foreign nations lying at anchor at Sacrificios, there were an English man-of-war brig, a French ditto, and a Spanish sloop of war. The officers of these vessels were all on the poop, or quarter-deck, and their crews on the rigging, all apparently eyeing our proceedings with much curiosity, as we came up and successively dropped anchor, our nearest vessels about a cable's length astern of them. The order of landing was to be as follows: General Worth was to land first with his division; General Twiggs was to land with the second division as soon as the boats returned from landing all of the first; General Scott with the third division was not to land until the following morning. As our regiment belonged to the second division, we had an excellent opportunity of witnessing the landing of the first party — an interesting spectacle, as we fully expected they would receive a warm reception from the Mexicans, who we imagined were stationed behind the sand-hills. A little above high-water mark, on the coast, in the neighbourhood of Vera Cruz, there is a series of sand-hills, formed by the drifting of the fine sand by the violent north gales that blow during the winter months. These sand-hills are thirty or forty feet to a hundred feet in height, the highest being in the vicinity of the city. It was on the highest of these that our batteries were erected for its bombardment. Immediately opposite where we were to land, they formed a sloping acclivity, varying from thirty to fifty feet in height, covered with short scrubby brushwood, and the prickly pear cactus. While the troops were getting into the landing-boats, an operation which, though using all possible despatch, occupied about half an hour, the gunboats sailed as close as they could to the shore, throwing an occasional shell into the brushwood, for the purpose of ascertaining if the Mexicans had any masked batteries erected, as we supposed. There being no indication of any enemy in the vicinity, and the boats being now filled, everything was ready for landing the first party.

I cannot say that I felt in the slightest degree inclined to earn high fame or distinction, by any very decided demonstration or

extraordinary exhibition of personal prowess and heroic valour
on the present occasion; neither did I overhear any very strong
expressions of regret amongst my comrades, at the circumstance of our regiment not being the first party who were landing. In a short conversation which the surgeon held with the
hospital attendant a few minutes before, we could overhear him
ask if the lint and bandages, and his case of instruments were
close at hand and immediately under his eye. An inquiry, just
at that particular juncture, horribly suggestive of thick-coming
fancies, and exceedingly well calculated to cool down any
dangerous excess of enthusiasm and martial ardor entertained
by those who overheard it. Still, when the boats, which contained fully two thousand men, were drawn up in line and
ready to start, so strong was the feeling of contagious sympathy elicited and communicated by the sight, surrounded as
it was by all the glorious pomp and circumstance of war, that
I believe there were few of the army who did not envy their
position, or would not gladly have incurred the hazard of the
enterprise, for the shadow of glory which the distinction conferred. The scene was certainly exciting and imposing: the
military bands of different regiments stationed on the decks of
the steamers, transports, and men-of-war, played the national
airs of "Yankee Doodle," "Hail Columbia," and the "Star
Spangled Banner." Ten thousand of our own troops were
anxious and eager spectators, and the English, French, and
Spanish fleets, had each their representative, scanning our operations with critical eye, and all looking with curiosity to see the
issue of the exploit.

At a signal from the vessel having General Scott on board,
the boats simultaneously gave way for shore, leaving a considerable space vacant in front of our men-of-war, who were
anchored next the shore, and had their guns double shotted,
ready to open upon the enemy, should they make their appearance. The gun-boats, meanwhile, continued to tack backwards
and forwards, almost close to the shore, for the same purpose.
Under the circumstances, it was plain that the Mexicans could

not prevent us from landing, but, by waiting until the first party were fairly on the sands, they might assault them with a very superior force, when our gun-boats and men-of-war would be prevented from firing, by the fear of injuring our own men. This was the event we almost expected to witness, and, as the boats neared the shore, all straining their energies for the honour of being the first to land, we watched the result with intense anxiety, expecting each moment to see a body of Mexican cavalry charge over the sand-hills. But no such event occurred; on coming to within about a hundred yards of the shore, the boats grounded on a small sandbar. The men and officers immediately leaped into the water, the former carrying their muskets on their shoulders, and holding their cartridge boxes well up, as the water reached to their hips while wading ashore. As the boats successively arrived, the men were formed on the beach; the boats making all expedition back to the vessels for more men. All of the first party having formed into line, several regimental colours were displayed, and a charge made to the heights in front, but not a single Mexican was to be seen. The American flag was immediately planted amidst loud and prolonged cheers, which were enthusiastically echoed by the troops on board. All idea of there being any fighting for that day, at least, was now at an end, piquets were thrown out, and sentries posted on the most advantageous points of the heights to guard against a surprise; the men began to make themselves at home; we could observe fires were kindled, and camp kettles swinging on them, in less than an hour after they had landed, and before evening the beach had all the appearance of a camp.

The captain of the *Porpoise* brig, who seemed a jovial and good-hearted fellow, proposing to act hospitably to the soldiers whom he had on board, ordered the steward to furnish an allowance of grog to each, the same as the sailors were in the habit of receiving; but our officers put a stop to the exercise of his generosity, for which extreme shabbiness they had the contempt of the captain, and the discontented murmurs of

their own men. Their conduct, on this occasion, was the more
freely commented on and censured, as it was well known that
they had all partaken of the captain's hospitality, without stint,
themselves, and it was utterly absurd to imagine that a single
allowance of grog could injure any person, however unused to
spirits. We had been standing on deck all day in the hot sun,
with our muskets in our hands, for there was neither an awning
nor room to sit down anywhere, on account of the crowded
state of the deck. It would probably be nine or ten o'clock
that night before we got ashore, when we should have to lie
down and sleep on the beach without taking off our accoutre-
ments, which we should have to wear for days, perhaps for
weeks to come. But all these disagreeables, as they were the
natural and unavoidable consequence of our position, were as
dust in the balance, compared with the reflection, that our
officers grudged us the slight degree of sympathetic consola-
tion, implied in the good-natured captain's offer of a glass of
grog. "The dirty miserly nagurs," audibly grumbled Micky
Ryan, "faith, an' six allowances some of the customers have in
their own insides; may the Lord look down on us, for we've
happened badly on them for gintlemin; shure there's not one
of the miserly crathurs has a heart as big as a grasshopper's."

About ten o'clock at night the boats came alongside to take
our regiment ashore, being the last of the second division. Two
or three lanthorns were held over the ship's side, and, the water
being smooth, we were soon all in.   We were then rowed
ashore till, the boat striking the sand, we had to jump in and
wade up to the middle for about a hundred yards, as the others
had done. This was a bad preparation for going to sleep on
the beach, but, except when there is a north gale blowing,
which was not the case that night, the night air is warm on the
beach of Vera Cruz, and we suffered little inconvenience from
our wetting. We were met by an officer on shore, who said
he would show us the position our regiment was to occupy;
and, after being formed into companies, we were marched along
the beach through a number of rows of small oblong heaps,

which, in the dim starlight, the sky being partially obscured by the drifting clouds, bore a striking, and I could scarce help fancying, ominous resemblance to an extensive and over-populous graveyard. At length we arrived at a vacant spot in the line which had been reserved for our occupation, and, having been directed to pile arms, we were told we might lie down when we pleased, but in the immediate vicinity of our arms, which each man was to be ready to grasp at a moment's notice. This was the first time I had ever seen a bivouac, and, certainly, it seemed a very primitive and cool way of lodging; as my comrade Nutt remarked, it did look rather like taking actual possession of the soil. After enjoying a comfortable smoke, we prepared for taking a warrior's rest, by wrapping our martial cloaks around us, or pulling the capes of our great-coats over our heads, to exclude the sand and night air; we tumbled over on the beach, and were soon several fathoms deep in the land of dreams.

But the Mexicans were not disposed to allow us the undisturbed possession of our first night's quarters, indifferent though they were, without giving an intimation, at least, of their sentiments towards us. It was between twelve and one o'clock, and only about an hour after we had fallen asleep, that we were roused by the report of musketry, and found the whole camp a scene of the utmost confusion and commotion. A number of the men, owing to the fatigue of the previous day, and having slept little the previous night, were so sound asleep, that it was only by violently shaking or kicking them, that they could be roused. At last they were all got up and formed into line, when we were directed to examine the priming of our muskets, and see if they were ready for immediate use. In the meantime the balls flew over our heads, with their peculiar metallic ringing sort of whistle, in quick succession; and, though high enough fortunately to do little damage, yet quite near enough to make nervous persons feel rather uncomfortable. The firing continued for about ten minutes, in as quick a succession of reports as would be made by the irregular file-firing of two or three hundred men; and, if it had been well directed, as it easily might have been, by an enemy well acquainted with the surrounding country, and the position we occupied, we might have paid dear for our "lodgings upon the cold ground." A few rounds from a division of infantry ordered out for the purpose, having caused these night disturbers to scamper, we soon piled arms, and in a few minutes were again fast asleep; and, thanks to the vigilance of our out-lying piquets, who gave and received a dropping fire until near morning, we enjoyed our slumbers unmolested during the remainder of the night. Next morning, we learned that the firing of the previous night had proceeded from a body of lancers from the city, who had been quickly driven in by a regiment of General Worth's division. The casualties of the night were five or six wounded, one or two of whom were, report said, dangerously hurt; but there had been none killed.

* * *

Early next morning, the third division, with the Commander-in-Chief, General Scott, landed; and our army having been formed into column, we moved to a position a mile or two nearer the town, and covered from observation by the sand-hills. Here we bivouacked in the vicinity of a small stream — General Scott and his staff had tents pitched — the remainder, officers as well as men, crept under the shade of the bushes to screen themselves from the scorching rays of the sun, or sticking stout branches upright in the ground, cut a quantity of leafy twigs to serve as a roof, and thus made a tolerable sort of a bower. In the meantime, one of our light batteries was out skirmishing with the enemy's outposts, which offering slight resistance, were successively driven in with little difficulty. From the landing of siege material and heavy ordnance, which had busily commenced, we now perceived that the intention of General Scott was to bombard the city.

A great deal of virtuous indignation has been exhibited by the English press on the subject of the bombardment of Vera Cruz, which it has generally stigmatized as a barbarous slaughter of women and children, having no parallel in modern history. It was asserted that Wellington, or any of his generals, had never bombarded an open city, and a great deal more of a similar tendency, all calculated to show that war is carried on in a highly humane and civilized mode by the enlightened nations of Europe; and that the Americans, and General Scott in particular, had behaved in a very barbarous manner. Now all that sort of twaddle seems excessively weak to any one at all acquainted with the circumstances; the truth being notorious that General Scott, besides being one of the most skilful and scientific generals of modern times, is also one of the most humane men in the world. For my part, I have not the slightest doubt that his character, in respect of the noblest attributes of humanity, may bear triumphant comparison with that of the most praiseworthy and philanthropic members of any society, order, or profession, in the world. The real fact being, that his humanity, and a desire to spare a needless effusion of blood, caused him to adopt the method he took for the reduction of Vera Cruz; being anxious to avoid a repetition of the horrible and savagely barbarous scenes consequent on the storming of a city, of which the history of the Peninsular war may furnish a few examples illustrative of the humane practices of European armies. To understand this apparent paradox, one should know a few of the facts of the case. In the first place, Vera Cruz, so far from being an open city, is very well fortified, having a wall and ditch all round it, and a series of half-moon batteries, not deficient in the requisite ordnance to make a stout resistance. These batteries sweep a perfectly level plain, extending from half a mile to a mile between the walls and the sand-hills, and would have proved very destructive to an assaulting party. Now, if the inhabitants, receiving, as they did, two or three weeks' previous notice to quit, preferred remaining in the city, General Scott having plainly signified that, for certain economical reasons, he declined taking their batteries with the bayonet, and intended to try a game at the long bowls, which the Mexicans are so fond of themselves — if being duly warned, they chose to remain and be killed, I do not see how General Scott should be blamed for the result. But let us suppose that, with the intention of sparing the lives of the inhabitants, by the very disinterested sacrifice of the lives of a few of the troops under his command, he had decided on carrying the place by assault, which would probably have cost the assaulting force from 1,000 to 1,500 men; does any person, in the possession of sound intellect, imagine that, in the latter event, General Scott could have prevented scenes of plunder, the resistance of inhabitants, and the commission of deeds of crime and horror, fearful to contemplate? Those who think that troops, even of well-disciplined armies (a character I would by no means claim for the army under General Scott), can be held in subordinate check by any amount of exertion on the part of their officers, on an occasion of the above nature, are not likely, I apprehend, to form a correct idea on the subject. But to any impartial person, taking an unprejudiced view of the case, I think it will appear tolerably obvious, that the method adopted by General Scott was the most humane even for the inhabitants.

A few days after landing, the various divisions were ordered to the positions which they were to occupy during the progress of the siege. The division to which I belonged, that of General Twiggs, was ordered to Vergara, a small village close to the sea-beach, and on the north-west side of the city, from which it was distant about four miles. In crossing a high sand-hill behind the city, our men being exposed to the view of one of their batteries, they kept up an incessant fire of round shot and shell while our division passed, which, being in file, occupied a considerable time; but they showed no great proficiency in gunnery on this occasion, as very few of their shot took effect. It was here that I heard, for the first time, the singular and diabolically-horrific sound which a large shell makes when passing within a short distance; I don't mean when it explodes (as that exactly resembles the noise made in firing a gun), but when it passes within a few, or it may be fifty or a hundred yards; the noise seeming equally loud and discordant in either case. I recollect a reply of honest Mick Ryan on being asked if he had ever heard a sound like that before. "No," said Mick, "one can both hear and feel that sound — by the Eternal, I felt it all over." There is no earthly sound bearing the slightest resemblance to its monstrous dissonance; the angriest shriek of the railway whistle, or the most emphatic demonstration of an asthmatic engine at the starting of a train, would seem like a strain of heavenly melody by comparison. Perhaps Milton's description of the harsh, thunder-grating of the hinges of the infernal gates, approaches to a faint realization of the indescribable sound, which bears a more intimate relation to the sublime than the beautiful. However, the Mexicans did very small damage by their practice; the only result was to make our men fall flat on the sand; which they did every time a shell came, and which I have no doubt saved a few limbs from damage. It was amusing, even amidst the danger from these horrid missiles, to see an officer, after getting up and anathematizing his men emphatically for lying down on the sand, drop as suddenly and as flat as any of them, when the next shell came whizzing rather close to him. The only victim to this ball-practice of the Mexicans in our regiment was a little drummer-boy, about thirteen years of age, named Rome, who had one of his arms shot off by the fragment of an exploding shell. He was one of the most quiet and obliging boys in the regiment, and we were all very sorry for him; many of the men saying if it had been such a boy (naming one of the others), it would have been no great matter, but it was a pity for poor little Rome. The little fellow cried very bitterly at the time, but the surgeon having carefully amputated it, he soon recovered, and on our regiment returning to New York in August, 1849, he came over to Governor's Island to see us. He was then living with a gentleman in New York, who employed him to carry messages and do light work for him. A captain of a volunteer regiment had his head taken off by a cannon-ball the same afternoon; but considering the immense amount of their practice, and the quantity of ammunition fired by their various batteries, the smallness of our loss in killed and wounded is astonishing: the total American loss including those killed and wounded in skirmishes in the vicinity of the city, during the whole siege, only amounted to seventeen killed and fifty-seven wounded.

We bivouacked near the edge of a thick *chaparral*, about four or five miles from Vergara, the position our division was to occupy; but which, for some reason or other, we did not move to for the next three days. We were amused with a volunteer whom we met here, coming out of the chaparral loaded with two muskets and a turkey. He had followed the turkey, a tame one, into the chaparral, and having strayed too far off the road, he was seen and fired at by a Mexican piquet — they exchanged a few shots, he said, when he killed the yellow beggar by shooting him through the body. He had brought the Mexican's musket as well as the turkey, a fine fat one, and decidedly the most valuable prize in general estimation; he spoke very contemptuously of the Mexican's skill in the use of fire-arms, none of his shots having come within yards of him. On quitting us, he added, that there were plenty more in the chaparral, and he guessed he would shoot another before sun-down; whether he meant turkey or Mexican was difficult to comprehend, but, as he seemed to enjoy the sport of shooting the one biped about as much as the other, I have no doubt he considered them both equally fair game. As usual, we were aroused during the night by the firing of musketry, and fell in under arms until the alarm was discovered to be false. These nocturnal alarms were very annoying for the first week or so after landing, as we never passed a night without being roused from our sleep, and ordered to fall in under arms, and this too, twice or thrice during the course of the night sometimes. At last, as they were found, except in one or two instances, to be caused by the blundering of sentries, a number of whom were Germans, and not sufficiently acquainted with the English language to clearly comprehend their orders, our officers ceased to mind these alarms; and when wakened by the report of a few muskets we only turned over to sleep again, grumbling a curse on the stupidity originating the disturbance. Bodies of the enemy, principally lancers, were known to be in the vicinity; but, owing to the nature of the country round Vera Cruz, which is covered with chaparral, no body of the enemy could approach our lines at night by any other mode than the open road. These keys of the position were well watched by our piquets, and being defended by a few field-pieces, there was little danger to be apprehended from an enemy like the one we had to contend with. A few desultory skirmishes took place between part of General Worth's division, consisting of volunteers, and Colonel Harney's dragoons, and a body of Mexican lancers; but the Mexicans fought very shy on these occasions, and soon gave up the idea of being able to effect anything like a bold stroke in favour of the besieged. For two or three days after moving from where we landed, all our provisions had to be carried from the beach, a distance of three or four miles through heavy sands, and under a scorching sun; and as the men who carried them had to take their arms at the same time, to defend themselves in case of an attack, the duty was excessively fatiguing. Several of our men who died shortly after, assigned as the cause of their illness, the over-exertion they had used when on these harassing fatigue duties.

Our supply of water while lying here was scanty and bad, being only procurable by digging holes in the sand to the depth of four or five feet, and then waiting until the muddy-looking fluid oozed up to a sufficient depth to enable us to dip it with the tin cups which we carried. We were all very glad, therefore, when we moved to Vergara, as we were told that there, at least, we should have plenty of good water. Our road at first wound through chaparral and tangled thickets of *cacti* and other war-like vegetables of the *chevaux de frise* order, along the edge of a marsh, where we halted in order to drink and fill our canteens with the water which it contained. As we had all been suffering considerably for the previous two days from the effects of thirst, few were inclined to criticise too nicely the quality of this water, which, though not exactly transparent, yet to observe the apparent gusto with which almost all quaffed repeated draughts of it, one might have fancied it to be exceedingly like nectar, indescribably sweet. "Hunger is a good sauce," says the proverb, and thirst is equally remarkable as a filter. We had a Mexican guide with us who was well acquainted with the country in the environs of the city, and who rode beside General Twiggs. In all our marches in Mexico, the guide always rode along with the commander of the division, acting as interpreter and guide both, upon occasion. When we approached within two miles of Vergara, our road led through a rich and fertile soil, partially cultivated, and containing a number of very large and venerable-looking trees. We also passed several *ranchos*, but all deserted by their owners, the poor creatures having been the first to suffer from our invasion. We soon reached Vergara, a few straggling huts on a road leading down to the beach. A beautiful clear stream emptied its waters into the sea close to the village, so clear that every motion of the small fish playing in its pellucid pools, was as distinctly visible as those of the unfortunate goldfish one sometimes observes pensively circumgyrating in the interior of its enchanted globular ball in the shop-window. The banks of the stream were shaded for miles by magnificent trees, and in the adjacent thickets a variety of wild fruits were found growing; but the only ones I found ripe were lemons and limes, of which I plucked quantities to squeeze in water, an acidulous drink being exceedingly refreshing with the thermometer upwards of ninety. When returning in July of the following year, I found some delicious guavas and sour sops in these thickets. The timber and the fertility of the soil are unusual features in the face of the country in the vicinity of Vera Cruz; for a considerable distance round which sandy hillocks and swampy morasses, varied by a section of dense chapparal, are the general rule. The chaparral, or natural thicket, of Mexico, is totally unlike any other thicket I have ever seen — a great portion of it being completely impenetrable. All the shrubs

and trees of the dense chaparral bear clusters of thorns, sharp
as the stings of bees, and as stubborn as bayonets. The various
tribes of the cactus nation, with their innumerable needles —
trifles in comparison to the thorns before mentioned — fill up
the intervals between the thorn-bearing trees, rendering the
whole a complete series of impregnable natural defences. The
foregoing description applies to thick or dense chaparral,
which is utterly impassable — of course, there are portions of
it more open, where thorny shrubs are less frequent, and which
may be traversed with ease.

We found a waggon loaded with barrels of Madeira wine
in the village — it had just arrived from Jalapa, and was destined for the garrison at Vera Cruz. General Twiggs ordered
the wine to be distributed amongst the men, and we each received a small measure containing about half-a-pint. General
Twiggs and his officers found good quarters in the huts of the
village — the different regiments bivouacking in the vicinity.
In the evening a report was current that a body of lancers
meant to attack us during the night, and the piquets had orders
to be on the alert. The road, at the distance of about a mile
from our encampment, was defended by two field-pieces, and a
few trees were felled and laid across the road, but the lancers
declined making their appearance.

Next day a schooner arrived loaded with provisions, saving
the men a very laborious task of carrying them round from
the beach. Still the duties of guards, piquets, and fatigue parties, harassed the men greatly; and many of them were soon
prostrated by disease — especially with that scourge of armies
on a campaign, diarrhoea. About a week after our arrival, we
also got tents pitched — our regimental baggage having been
brought round from Sacrificios by light sailing vessels. Our
knapsacks also arrived at the same time; but the plight in which
we received them, was the cause of loud and general complaint;
many of them being rifled of their most valuable contents, and
some completely gutted, while but a small number had escaped

untouched. They had been left on the beach, at the place where we had landed, for the previous eight or ten days, during which time they had been in charge of different hordes of volunteers, who, as might have been expected, had made rather too free with their contents. But there was no help for it; and the bursting choler of many found vent in a storm of imprecations and maledictions, while the more cool and reflective only hoped they would have an opportunity of serving out a volunteer before the end of the campaign.

* * *

A singular coincidence with the prediction of the insane sailor who came to Tampico with us in the John Potter, occurred while we lay at Vergara. This was the total loss of that brig, which, with two schooners sent round from Sacrificios with stores and provisions, was driven ashore by one of those violent north gales which blow so frequently on this coast during the winter. There being no practicable means of getting them off, without incurring more expense than they were worth, they were left to their fate; and when we returned in the summer of the following year, their upright timbers protruded from the sand, where they lay firmly imbedded. Several of our men considered the occurrence ocular demonstration of the existence of witchcraft, or some species of demonology, and some whom the march of intellect had rendered sceptical on these points had their faith in these ancient doctrines revived and confirmed.

The preparations for the bombardment of the city meanwhile went on vigorously, but many of the men appeared to think that General Scott was only losing time, and that a rush on the city at all points, to carry it by a *coup de main*, would be the only proper and effectual plan of proceeding. General Twiggs himself had been heard to express his disapproval of losing so much time, after the following manner, "Ugh! my boys'll have to take it yet with their bayonets." As a short description of General Twiggs may not be altogether uninteresting, I will give it as it struck me at the time. In height the General is about five feet ten inches, very broad shouldered and bull-necked, and is altogether a very stout and robust-looking man, though verging on sixty years of age. His face is large and red, with blue eyes, and rather coarse and heavy-looking features; an exuberant mass of tow-white hair, with long beard, and whiskers of the same colour, give him a gruff appearance, quite in keeping with his character, in which the disagreeable and the unprepossessing are the preponderating qualities. But he was a great favourite amongst the men, who admired him principally, I believe, for his brusquerie and coarseness of manner, and a singular habit he had of swearing most vehemently, and flying into a passion on the most trifling occasions. But though General Twiggs had the most republican contempt for etiquette, and even the common courtesies of civilized life, in his intercourse with others, he was furious if a soldier happened to omit paying him the customary military salute in passing.

The erection of the batteries on the sand hills, and the con-veyance of so much heavy ammunition to places convenient, was a very laborious task for our army in such a warm and exhausting climate. But all the troops took their share of the duty, each regiment working so many hours in succession, under its officers. At last, by dint of prodigious and untiring exertion, parties of our men having been employed in working day and night ever since our landing, on the 22nd of March, all being ready for operations, the town was formally summoned, and the governor having refused to surrender, the work of havoc and destruction was ordered to be commenced. For three successive days and nights, with short periods of inter-mission, the thunders of our guns and mortars, and the enemy's batteries in the city, were most deafening and incessant. On a height near our camp at Vergara, a number of our men fre-quently stood watching the shells at night; their appearance resembled that of the meteors called shooting or falling stars; and they were distinctly visible from the time when they began to ascend in their circling course until they disappeared among the roofs of the buildings. At length, on the 26th, after shot and shell to the number of seven thousand of those destructive missiles had been poured into the unfortunate city, they displayed a white flag, and after a day or two spent in negotiating, the following terms were finally agreed on. The town and castle were to be surrendered on the 29th, the garrison to march out of the central city gate and lay down their arms, and to be furnished with four days' provisions. The officers to be allowed to retain their arms, and to have five days to return to their native homes; all public property and *matériel* of war to belong to the American forces, the sick and wounded to be allowed to remain in the city, and no private property or building to be taken possession of by the Americans. On the 29th, the Mexicans, amounting to between four and five thousand, marched out of the city, and deposited their arms in front of a strong body of the American army drawn up to receive them. A brigade under General Quitman marched in and occupied the garrisons forthwith, and the American flag floated over San Juan d'Ulloa and the city of Vera Cruz.

Having procured a written permission from the officer commanding our regiment, a few days after our troops had taken possession of the city, I visited it in company with Sergeants Lear and Beebe, of ours; being curious to observe the effects of the bombardment, and also to gratify our curiosity with a view of the interior of a city which at a short distance presents a very grand and imposing appearance. The city of Vera Cruz is very well built, the houses being of stone, and the walls of the most substantial thickness, an excellent thing in a warm climate. The streets are wide and well paved, and its general appearance is that of a clean, neat, and compactly built city. It contains a number of very handsome churches, the painted and gilt domes of which give a highly imposing effect to the view of it from a short distance. The interiors of several of these churches which we visited were highly ornamented with shrines, and all the profusion of carving, gilding, and painting,

usual in these places; the most of it tawdry and vulgar-looking
I imagined. One of the churches which we entered near the
centre of the city, the most richly decorated we have seen,
having a fine marble-paved floor, a magnificent dome, and
some very good pictures, had been converted into an hospital
for the wounded, and contained upwards of a hundred male
patients at the time we were in it. Several shells had fallen
through the dome, on the marble floor, the fragments of which
had made sad mutilations of the pictures and effigies of the
saints and virgins of the various shrines round the building.
And what seemed to us heretics far more pitiable, though
doubtless of minor importance in the eyes of a true Catholic,
one of these shells had killed and wounded about twenty of
the unfortunate inhabitants who had fled to its shelter as a
sanctuary of safety during the bombardment. The whole of
the south-west side of the city, which, lying nearest our batteries, was most exposed to the storm of destructive missiles,
was a scene of desolation calculated to make the most strenuous
advocates of physical force pause and reflect. For my own
part, while ready to admit the whole weight and force of such
powerful arguments, I felt strongly inclined to doubt the justice or propriety of having recourse to them. Whole streets
were crumbled to ruins, and they told us the killed and
wounded inhabitants amounted to between five and six hundred, while the soldiers who had been employed at their batteries during the whole time of the bombardment had as many
more; the entire killed and wounded being over a thousand.

CHAPTER 13

They Have Unconditionally Surrendered

On March 29, 1847, the formal surrender of Vera Cruz took place. "Genl. Scott deserves, and I hope will receive, all credit with his countrymen for the almost bloodless triumph," insisted an artillery officer. "God grant that this may lead to an arrangement by which this unfortunate war may be closed." How the Americans had won this great victory was explained in a letter from Captain George Archibald McCall (1803–1868), written after the occupation of Vera Cruz.

CAPTAIN GEORGE ARCHIBALD MCCALL
Letters from the Frontiers
Philadelphia, J. B. Lippincott & Co., 1868, pp. 483–484

March 28, 1847

MY DEAR M——:

Bien, c'est une affaire! — the crisis is past; they have unconditionally surrendered the City and the Castle. I can scarcely realize the thing. We had not twenty-five pieces in battery until the last day, mortars and battering-pieces; yet the city with seventy-five heavy guns, and the castle with two hundred and fifty, in battery, have yielded; and their garrisons, near 5000 men, yield themselves prisoners of war. The latter are to march out to-morrow at ten o'clock A.M., and lay down their arms. One month ago, as we were leaving Tampico, the general impression of the officers of the army was that we should have a hard struggle, and it was not calculated that the reduction of their strong places would be effected at a less cost than 2000 men. The God of battles has fought with us, for our entire loss does not exceed forty men killed and wounded; whereas the loss of the enemy is acknowledged to be very great. The destruction of property in the city is excessive; two-thirds of the houses are represented to be much shattered. The town was fired by our shells many times; but the roof of almost every house is of tiles, so that the conflagration did not spread after destroying the interior of the house into which the shell had fallen and exploded. But our mortar batteries fired so rapidly, that at night you might see the shells in a constant stream, following each other into the devoted place; and as they fell, crash after crash indicated the certain and constant work of destruction. Men were dashed to pieces while the surgeons were dressing their wounds; numbers were left howling where they fell. And no retreat was a shelter from this horrid shower of bursting shells. Their yells and screams were heard by ourselves and by our people from one end of the town to the other. Alas! many poor inoffensive creatures suffered with the combatants in this indiscriminate slaughter; and it is grievous, indeed, to relate, that a young lady, the daughter of the British Consul, was killed by a shell that struck his house. I am told that he says he blames no one but himself. He should have left the city, as almost all the families did; but he believed his house bomb-proof.

Our batteries were at work but three days and a half; but the troops, while completing the investment of the city, and while advancing our own works, were almost constantly by day, and occasionally by night, under the fire of the enemy's guns for seventeen days. None of our camps except perhaps General Scott's Headquarters, which also was now and then reached, were out of the range of their guns, and the only thing to be wondered at, is the trifling loss we sustained. I have repeatedly seen an eighteen-pounder shot strike in the midst of a dozen or twenty men without injuring one of them. This kind of thing *did* occur so often at all points of our line, that it is scarcely credible to those who were standing by, and is a frequent subject of conversation among all ranks.

An expedition, land and naval, sets out on the 30th against Alvarado, that much abused place. Brig.-General Quitman, of this division, goes by land; who is to command the naval force, I have not yet learned. A portion of the forces will also march towards the interior as soon as the means of transporting ammunition and provisions can be collected. It is now thought that General Taylor's victory, and the fall of this place, will induce the towns on our march to the city of Mexico, to open their gates as we approach.

I have seized a moment almost every day to scratch off a line or two to you, as I supposed you would feel an interest in our operations.

I have only to add that I am quite well, and ready for anything that may turn up. Adieu.

CHAPTER 14   How Far Shall
                We Charge?

Vera Cruz provided the base needed for Scott's projected
movement into central Mexico, but the city was a dangerous
place for American troops in warm weather. The dreaded
vómito, or yellow fever, was a constant threat in the spring
and summer. An epidemic might destroy the army. So Scott
hurried his preparations, and early in April his forces marched
out of the city and up the National Highway toward Jalapa
and Mexico City. Private George Ballentine described the
march as well as the battles along the way.

PRIVATE   GEORGE   BALLENTINE
Autobiography of an English Soldier in the United States Army
New York, Stringer & Townsend, 1853, pp. 167–169, 171–264

. . . A great deal of sickness prevailing among the troops,
General Scott wisely determined to lose no time in removing
the main body to Jalapa, where it was said to be his intention
to wait for further reinforcements from the States. General
Twiggs with his division was to march on the 7th of April, the
other two divisions following in succession. As an engagement
with the enemy was anticipated before we reached Jalapa, and
as the means of transport were too limited to admit of our

carrying much of our baggage along with us, all the heaviest of it, together with our tents, was directed to be packed up and left in the quartermaster's stores at Vera Cruz. A great number of sick were left behind, few of whom ever joined again, as most of the poor fellows soon fell victims to the unwholesome climate and the careless treatment soldiers receive in over-crowded hospitals during a campaign. Among those early victims for whom we were especially sorry, were Davies and Bob Madden, formerly mentioned, who were left behind with several more of our company, and of whose deaths we received intimation shortly after we arrived at Jalapa.

On the morning of the 7th, about seven o'clock, our division, consisting of about 3000 infantry, a light battery, consisting of two six-pounder field pieces and two twelve-pounder howitzers, and a small body of cavalry, proceeded on our march to Jalapa. For the first six or seven miles our progress was very slow and painful, the road being a loose sand, in which we sank to the ankles at every step. A great many of the men, myself among the number, were ill with diarrhoea; but being of opinion that small chance of renewed health awaited those who stayed behind in the hospitals at Vera Cruz, we were all glad to get away from it; trusting for a renewal of our exhausted vigour to the purer air of the mountains, which a few days' march would enable us to breathe. After marching about three miles, we halted at a bridge thrown over a small stream which crossed the road, and many of the men taking off their knapsacks, began to select those articles which they resolved to carry, throwing the remainder away. Numbers of them reserved only a great-coat or blanket, deliberately sacrificing the rest of their effects, and before we reached Santa Fé, a small village about eight miles from Vergara, the road was strewn with articles of clothing thrown away by the men.

We halted in the village of Santa Fé, for a short time, and General Twiggs and the officers of his staff entered a house where they sat down to rest, sheltered from the scorching heat

of the sun. Some of the men in the meantime had discovered
an apartment at the other end of the building, containing some
barrels of aquadiente, or Mexican brandy, and an entrance having been effected, a considerable portion of the liquor had
found its way into the men's canteens, before a knowledge of
their proceedings had been communicated by the Mexican to
the General. The anger of General Twiggs as he rushed to the
scene, and the celerity with which the marauders "*vamosed
the ranche*," as they heard the ominous alarm of "here's old
Davy," transcend description. Two or three of the unlucky
wights, however, he met on the threshold of the door, on their
way out; these he seized by the collar and swung round till he
had an opportunity of administering a sound kick to their
posteriors. None of them, however, stayed to remonstrate on
these rather unpleasant demonstrations of the old General's
love of justice, being only too happy to get out of that fix so
easily, and the bugle having been ordered to sound "The As-
sembly," we were formed into our ranks, and the march was
immediately resumed.

General Twiggs, who rode at the head of the division, committed a great error in permitting the men in front to walk too
quick on this day's march. The consequence of this was that
a great many of the men being weak from the effects of diarrhoea could not keep up, and slipped off the road into the
thickets, which after leaving Santa Fé began to offer an inviting
shade, and in which many of them lay down and deliberately
resolved on staying behind the division. When we reached the
place where we were to encamp for the night, a small stream
about five miles from Santa Fé, the rear of the column was
several miles behind, the men straggling along the road at their
own discretion; and when the rolls were called at sunset, about
a third of the men were absent, not having come up. We
bivouacked under the trees by the roadside, the grass was deliciously soft and elastic, and, after a supper of coffee, biscuit,
and pork, Nutt made us some aquadiente punch, after quaffing

a bumper or two of which, we lay down, and slept very comfortably until roused by the *reveille* next morning about four
o'clock.

. . . Some of the men who had fallen behind came up with
us this evening. They said the rest of the stragglers had determined not to come up with the division for a few days: They
had shot some cattle, and were plundering the houses of those
who sold aquadiente of that article, as they came along; and
upon the whole they seemed to be taking pretty good care of
themselves; at all events these demonstrations seemed tolerably
vigorous for sick and delicate persons unable to keep up with
the division. Most of them came up with General [Robert]
Patterson's division, which was only one day's march behind
us, and except a few who were killed by the peasantry, they
had all joined before the battle of Cerro Gordo.

We commenced the next day's march about an hour before
sunrise, as we wished to have the most of it over before the
extreme heat of noon. The road was up hill, rocky, and very
bad travelling for man or beast; it also lay through a barren
tract of country, and water was not to be procured. Those
men who had neglected to fill their canteens with water before
starting, found great difficulty in procuring a drink when
thirsty to-day; as the others who had been more provident,
considered it sufficient hardship to carry enough for themselves.
At length, about 11 o'clock, on winding down a steep hill, we
came in sight of the *Puente Nacional* (National Bridge). This
was the first scene since we had entered Mexico, that by its
picturesque beauty called forth a spontaneous burst of admiration. "Scotland or d——n me," was the exclamation of Jock
Whitelaw, a Glasgow callant, as the scene opened on his delighted vision. The precipitous banks of the river, rocky, and
ornamented with tufts of flowering shrubs, shooting out from
its fissures, and suggestive of broom and breckan, blue bells
and heather, render the scene exceedingly like the section of a
Scotch river glen. Indeed, I believe the most unimaginative
Scotchman will hardly pass the National Bridge without feeling

his native land suggested to memory by the similar character-istics of the scenery. The bridge is a very substantial and magnificent-looking structure, built of stone arches through which rushes the clear and rapid stream over a fine pebbly channel. We halted here a considerable time, for the purpose of allowing the men to refresh themselves with the delicious sparkling water of the Rio Antiqua (Old River). We then marched through a village of huts which stood on each side of the road at the end of the bridge, the walls of which were canes, and wooden poles, made into a sort of hurdles, and the roofs thatched with palm leaves. The village was shaded by some very fine mimosas, and on a plain at the end of it we encamped for the night. The weather had been fine since we left Vera Cruz, and we had suffered no inconvenience from sleeping on the grass; my health had also materially improved, a result I had anticipated from the exercise of marching, which had always agreed with me. In the afternoon, my comrade Nutt and myself went down to the river and bathed, after which we washed our shirts and stockings, which soon dried in the hot sunshine. We remarked, while going through the village, that all the huts except two or three containing a few old women and children, were empty and deserted. This was considered a proof that a force was collected at some point farther on the road, and between us and Jalapa.

We commenced our march before sunrise next morning as usual, and after a fatiguing march over a tolerably good road, but mostly up hill, and with thick woods on each side of it, which obscured the view and prevented the circulation of air, we arrived about twelve o'clock at *Plan del Rio* (The River of the Plain). At the entrance to the village, we crossed a fine bridge of hewn stone, thrown over a broad and rapid, but shallow stream, with broken and precipitous banks, covered with a rich and luxuriant vegetation. The village, a wretched collection of huts, of similar construction to those at the National Bridge, was also deserted by its inhabitants. A party of lancers who were there when our advance guard, composed of a troop of dragoons, arrived, were very near being surprised and made prisoners. They had barely time to ride off pursued by our dragoons, with whom they exchanged a few shots, but owing to their horses being fresh, while our men's were tired with a long march, they soon increased the distance between them. These were an advanced piquet of the enemy, and we now knew that we were approaching close to their position. We encamped at the end of the village, and in the evening strong piquets were posted on the road in the direction of the enemy, ascertained to be only a few miles from Plan del Rio on the highway to Jalapa, which ascended a steep hill near the bottom of which we were encamped.

Our reconnoitring parties soon discovered that the enemy, who were in strong force, were in a position exceedingly well fortified, both by nature and art, to oppose our hitherto triumphant progress. On the highway to Jalapa, about four miles from Plan del Rio, the road enters a gorge between two heights, which the enemy had strongly fortified. About three quarters of a mile further, on the right-hand side of the road, rises the steep conical hill of Cerro Gordo, the key to the seemingly impregnable pass; as, in the event of our succeeding in forcing the other batteries, it, from its position and elevation, commanded both them and the intermediate road. This hill of Cerro Gordo, the Mexicans had also strongly fortified, and with the redoubtable Santa Anna commanding in person, and a force supposed to be at least fourteen or fifteen thousand strong, we all looked for some rather serious work, before luxuriating on the delicious fruits of Jalapa. To say that I felt no apprehension of personal danger at the prospect of an engagement likely to prove a severe one, would be ridiculous affectation; as I believe no man, possessing a particle of reflection, ever contemplated a similar position with perfect indifference. Be that, however, as it may, it seemed sufficiently evident to me on the present occasion, as well as on subsequent ones of a similar kind, that on the night before the expected engagement the camp wore an air of stillness unusual at other times, the men generally appearing more thoughtful, and conversing less, and in more subdued tones than usual.

On the evening of the 13th, General Twiggs, who, during the sickness of General Patterson, commanded the forces at Plan del Rio, after having spent two days in reconnoitring, gave the order for an attack on the enemy's batteries, which we were to take at the point of the bayonet by assault, early next morning. The bugle having sounded for the troops to assemble a little before sunset, the captains of companies addressed their men, informing them of the General's intention, and explaining as much of the plan of the meditated attack as would tend to facilitate its execution. They concluded with a hope that all would do their duty gallantly, and required us to give three cheers, an invitation which was very faintly responded to. The want of enthusiasm displayed by the men, arose, I am persuaded, from a want of confidence in the judgment of General Twiggs, and not from any deficiency of the necessary pluck required for the occasion. But that General, though always admitted to be a brave old cavalry officer, was considered, from his peculiar temperament, and previous school of education and discipline, to be totally incapable of successfully directing an operation of such magnitude as the present, which any person might easily see required both military talent and skill. Perfectly aware of the enemy's overwhelming force, and the strong nature of his position, and also of the inconsiderate rashness of General Twiggs and his advisers, we felt that we were in danger of a defeat, or a victory purchased by a lavish and useless expenditure of life. And as we knew that General Scott with a division of the army was only two days in rear, no one could perceive the least necessity for either of these alternatives; from either of them, however, we were fortunately saved.

It coming to the ears of General Patterson that an attack was ordered next morning, he immediately resumed the command of the troops by having his name erased from the sick returns. He then issued an order countermanding that of General

Twiggs, and stating that all active operations against the enemy's position were suspended until the arrival of General Scott. This turn of affairs gave universal satisfaction, as General Scott deserved and possessed the confidence of both officers and men in the highest degree. We had received a pint of flour each man for our next day's bread, the biscuit having all been consumed which we had brought with us; and it was considered better to make cakes and toast them on the ashes, than to go without bread all next day. When the news of General Patterson's order came as late as 11 o'clock at night, various groups of anxious-looking faces might be seen by the flickering light of the bivouac fire, gloomily watching their unleavened cakes, and thinking bitterly of the morrow. The announcement produced one of the most sudden illuminations of the human countenance divine among these groups, which I ever recollect to have seen; the cakes were either abandoned, or carried away half baked, to be finished at some other opportunity, and all retired to sleep, carrying the news to their dreaming comrades, that the attack was deferred until Scott came up.

*   *   *

On the 14th about noon, greatly to the satisfaction of us all, General Scott arrived with the rear division. We now expected that something would soon be done, and all seemed to feel a revival of confidence and anticipations of success. The gallant old General was loudly cheered on his arrival, and without waiting for rest or refreshment after his toilsome march, he immediately proceeded to reconnoitre the enemy's position. The result was the discovery of a ravine leading to the right of the enemy's batteries, by which it was resolved that the main attack should be made. At the bottom of this ravine was the celebrated hill of Cerro Gordo, of a conical form, and rising to a height of about two hundred feet from the plain. It had about a dozen brass guns, of small calibre, being principally six and nine pounders. Bounding the ravine on the left, there was another hill about as high as Cerro Gordo, the summits of the two hills being not more than half a mile distant. This hill, which General Scott determined to possess, was only covered by a piquet of the enemy, and could be easily obtained when required.

The 15th and 16th were occupied in a strict scrutiny of the enemy's works, and in removing obstacles to the passage of guns, ammunition, and troops, by cutting the obstructing trees and bushes. This was done by the pioneers, protected by a strong skirmishing party. On the evening of the 16th, we were ready for commencing serious operations.

It was a beautiful night at Plan del Rio on the 16th of April, 1847, and though on lying down to sleep one could see the lustrous stars shining in the blue canopy over head, yet we were in the "*Tierres calientes*" (the warm country), and one can sleep out of doors there very well in dry weather. Comfort, like everything else, has many degrees of comparison; for two or three nights previous we had a little more rain than was agreeable, one advantage of which was, that we now actually enjoyed a good night. "Sweet are the uses of adversity." Most of us therefore slept soundly until roused next morning from our slumbers by the reveille, which sounded about half-past four o'clock. Having taken a good breakfast of our usual camp fare — biscuit, beef, and coffee — the last meal for many a poor fellow, we prepared for the march by falling into our places in the ranks.

The division to which I belonged, consisting of about 3000 infantry, had orders to proceed under the command of General Twiggs, to take possession of the hill at the bottom of the ravine, and opposite Cerro Gordo, which General Scott had previously decided upon taking. It was covered by a piquet of the enemy whom we had orders to drive in, and retain the hill in possession, as upon it was considered to depend our best chance of success in our attack upon Cerro Gordo.

Having stowed away our knapsacks in the waggons which were left behind in the camp, with the other two divisions, we began our march up the hill. We expected to be engaged in a

slight skirmish with the enemy's piquets, but did not expect to
get into the thick of a regular engagement until next day. Still
a sort of chill was thrown over the spirits of most of the men;
jests which yesterday would have elicited roars of applausive
laughter, somehow seemed to hang fire this morning; and one
or two of our regimental wits being snubbed by meditative
officers for talking in the ranks, gave their vocation up in disgust, and became as gloomy and as taciturn as the others. It
was no great wonder either that the men were rather more
reflective than usual, considering that very few of our number
had ever been close in front of an enemy before, and we were
approaching fortifications which we should have to carry by
assault, at whatever sacrifice of life.

On coming to the head of the ravine, we were ordered to
form in file, trail arms, and keep perfect silence, the staff and
field officers dismounting and leading their horses. One of our
men happening to stumble over a stone, and his musket making
a loud clattering noise against his tin canteen, a captain rushes
up to him in the utmost fury, and bawls out loud enough to
be heard along the whole line, "You infernal scoundrel, I'll run
you through if you don't make less noise." As Blunderbore, for
that was a sobriquet the men had conferred on the captain,
stood flourishing his sword in a striking and theatrical attitude,
while the poor fellow seemed terrified lest he should put his
threat into execution, the scene presented such a ludicrous
aspect, that in spite of our proximity to the Mexican batteries,
all of us within sight and hearing burst into a hearty and simultaneous laugh.

Since 7 o'clock in the morning, when we first began to
ascend the hill from Plan del Rio, we had only gained three or
four miles, and it was now past noon. But we had moved very
slowly, every now and then halting half an hour or so, while
the rifles, as skirmishers, cautiously felt the way through the
chaparral in advance. The regiment to which I belonged, the
1st Artillery, was at the head of the column; we should therefore have the precedence in the series of military balls about to

be offered us by the Mexicans — a distinction I dare say not much valued by ourselves, or greatly coveted by others; the post of honour is sometimes the post of danger.

It was about 2 o'clock when we heard a few musket shots in front, followed by the sharp crack of our rifles, who had got within range of the advanced line of piquets. We immediately got the word to close up, and move in quick time to the front, and in a few minutes we were at the bottom of the hill occupied by the enemy. "First Artillery and Rifles form into line, and charge up the hill," was the word of command now given by General Twiggs. "I beg pardon, General, how far shall we charge them?" I heard one of our captains ask, as we hastily scrambled up. "Charge them to h—ll," was the reply of the rough old veteran, who remained with the rest of the division at the bottom of the hill. The balls came whistling in no very pleasant manner as we made our way up the steep hill, helping ourselves occasionally by the branches of the bushes; but the Mexicans are bad shots, and besides they were afraid to expose themselves by coming forward to take deliberate aim; so that all their balls went whistling over our heads, doing us no damage whatever. In the meantime on we went, shouting and hurrahing as if we were going to some delightful entertainment, every one in a state of the highest excitement, and nearly out of breath with hurrahing and running up the steep hill, but at the same time disdaining to think of stopping to recover it.

Before we reached the top of the hill, which we did with very trifling loss, the Mexicans quickly retreated down the opposite side of it, and now were experienced the bad effects of General Twigg's expression, "Charge them to h—ll." After obtaining possession of the hill, our object, I suspect, should have been to retain it in possession with the least possible amount of loss — General Scott having resolved to plant two twenty-four pounders on it during the night, and to open a fire early next morning on the battery at Cerro Gordo, and upon that side of the hill which he intended we should carry by assault. The summit of the hill is nearly half a mile distant from that of Cerro Gordo, and they are separated by a deep and rugged ravine. Our men were extended about half-a-mile along the face of the hill, firing upon the retreating Mexicans, with whom, in the eagerness of pursuit, we had become almost mixed up as we pursued them down the ravine. But when the enemy had got half-way up the opposite hill of Cerro Gordo, we saw the error we had committed in pursuing them, being now caught in a complete fix.

To attempt to retreat up the hill in the face of the continuous fire of some thousands of Mexican infantry, and that of their batteries, who now opened a crossfire (those to the left sweeping the side of the hill with round shot, and that of Cerro Gordo opposite pouring in volleys of grape and canister), would have been instant and total destruction. We were forced to remain therefore under the cover of rocks and trees, firing an occasional shot at the enemy only, who kept up an incessant, though fortunately for us a very ill-directed fire until near sunset. Indeed the loud and incessant roll of musketry all that afternoon, exceeded anything of the kind I ever heard. At length, towards sunset, the enemy seemed preparing for a grand charge; there was a cessation of firing nearly; we could observe their officers forming their men into the ranks, and with colours displayed, and a band of music playing in front, they at last advanced towards our position, which at that moment seemed sufficiently perilous. We had a small howitzer, of the kind called mountain howitzers, from their peculiar convenience in mountain warfare, for which they were expressly made; being light, and easily dismounted and carried up a hill. This was prepared for their reception, being well loaded with grape, and we waited with some anxiety to see its effects. On they came till near the bottom of the ravine, and within two or three hundred yards of us, when the howitzer sent its murderous contents among them. I never saw such sudden havoc and confusion caused by a single shot. It swept right into the head of the advancing column, killing and wounding a great number of those in advance, among others several of the band, who ceased playing the moment the shot struck the column, which halted almost instantly. "Arrah, more power to the hand that fired you, my jewel of a *how-its-yure;* it's yourself sure that knows how to pay the piper; that'll make you change your tune any how, you yellow pagans," cried Mickey Ryan. The Mexicans were thoroughly taken by surprise by this shot, and had quickly resolved not to risk another, for taking up their wounded they immediately began to retire to their former position. Except a straggling shot now and then, the firing on both sides soon ceased; it was getting dusk, and our men began to make their way to the main body by circling round the hill. Parties were now sent out to search for and carry in the wounded; but owing to the nature of the ground, and the darkness of the night, with a share of culpable neglect on the part of those whose duty it was to see the search more carefully prosecuted, I am afraid a number of the wounded perished, who might have recovered if they had been promptly attended to. I saw one poor fellow brought in after the battle next morning, who had been wounded and left on the field on the previous night, and who affirmed that there were groans of wounded men in all directions round him during the night.

I was witness to an incident this afternoon during the action, which for the diabolical spirit displayed by one of its actors exceeds anything of the kind I ever saw. An orderly sergeant named Armstrong, having received a wound in some part of the body, sat down seemingly in great agony. One of the men belonging to his own company came over to where he was sitting, and asked him if he was wounded; on his answering that he was, very badly, "Arrah, then may the devil cure ye, you black-hearted rascal," was the unfeeling rejoinder. The sergeant was not popular, and I believe his conduct was not calculated to inspire much sympathy for his misfortunes; but the wretch who could thus triumph in his physical sufferings and agony, must have been a fiend, and his conduct was very severely reprobated and commented on by his comrades. This diabolical spirit was engendered, by what is singularly enough called religious hatred; the sergeant having been an *Orangeman*, and the man addressing him a Roman Catholic. The sergeant died on the field that night, his watch and a purse containing some money, which he had on his person, were missing, and there were several bayonet wounds in his body. It was generally supposed that the Mexicans had killed and plundered him, as he had been left near their lines; but some did not hesitate to express their suspicions of foul play, and plainly intimated their belief that some of his own company had killed and robbed him.

When the action commenced, as we were scrambling up the hill, and while the balls were whistling rather thick in our vicinity, I felt a rather smart blow on the right temple. On the instant I imagined I had received a *quietus*, but a moment's reflection showed me that I was happily mistaken. The false alarm had arisen from the sudden recoil of a branch caused by a man a pace or two in advance, who was crushing through the brushwood, a branch of which in recoiling had struck me on the temple. The impression only lasted for a second, but I shall not soon forget the singular, and by no means pleasant, sensation caused by this simple occurrence.

Some men have blamed General Twiggs for leaving the remainder of the division inactive, while the small body sent to drive in the piquets were in such a dangerous predicament; but there I think he acted with good judgment. Had he engaged the whole division, he might have extricated the first party, but assuredly with a far greater sacrifice of life. Nothing but the paucity of our numbers, paradoxical as it may seem, saved us from a general slaughter on the occasion, enabling us to obtain the cover, of which a large body could not have equally availed themselves. The great fault which I, in common with all my comrades with whom I have conversed on the topic, think he committed, was that he did not give more explicit instructions to the officers in command of companies sent out on that occasion. Perhaps he did not clearly comprehend the instructions he had received from General Scott himself. At all events that a blunder had been made was evident, that it had cost us nearly two hundred men equally so, but no one thought of General Scott in connection with it. General Twiggs has all the credit of the first day of the battle of Cerro Gordo.

It was now dark, with a slight rain, and amidst the groans of the suffering wounded, who were having their wounds dressed, and amputations performed until late at night, the most smooth and soft piece of turf having been selected for their accommodation, tired and weary, we lay down to seek repose, and recruit our strength for the struggle of next morning. I had the bad fortune to be on a piece of ground which was full of small stones, but as we were ordered to keep our places as if in the ranks, in case of a night attack, I could not better it by shifting my ground. Still I managed to pick up a considerable number of them, and at last I found that it was somewhat more endurable. There was not much conversation amongst us this night, but taking a few mouthfuls of biscuit, a drink of water, and a smoke, we made ourselves as comfortable as, under the circumstances, was possible. As tending to show the effect of hardship and danger in blunting that feeling of subservient humility usually shown by the private soldier to his officer, I recollect an incident that occurred in the vicinity of where I was lying. One of our lieutenants sent a sergeant to a man of the name of Rielly whom he saw smoking, with a request for a smoke of his pipe. "Arrah, sweet, is your hand in a pitcher of honey, my jewel?" said Rielly; "the lieutenant is mighty condescending. May be you would be pleased, sergeant, to inform the lieutenant, along with Rielly's compliments, that if he will wait till Rielly has his own smoke — may the holy Virgin be near us, may be it's the last smoke ever the same Rielly will take — and tell Mickey Ryan, who axed the pipe afore him, has had a turn of it, I'll not be agin lending him the pipe." "Faith ye hae sent the sergeant aff wi' a flea in his lug," said a broad-spoken countryman of mine of the name of Findlay. "Bad luck to the impidence of the rapscallions, sure it's a gag they would be after putting in my mouth in the place of a pipe, if I was to ask one of themselves for a loan of the same thing," was the rejoinder of Teddy Rielly.

There was no disguising the fact that we had an ugly job before us next morning; but we had strong ground for hope in the positive cowardice of the Mexicans, our own comparative courage, and the superlative skill of General Scott. Besides, we had come through the baptism of fire that day, and were still unhurt, and perhaps we should be equally fortunate the next.

During the night, while we slept, the guns (two twenty-four pounders, with a complement of ammunition) had with incredible exertions been got to the summit of the hill, and placed in position for opening upon Cerro Gordo next morning. A temporary breastwork of stones and earth, capable of affording considerable protection to the men who would work them, had also been thrown up. I slept most uneasily all night, being cold and sore with lying on the stones; we had left our blankets and great-coats in the baggage waggons, and it had rained a little. I was not sorry therefore that when day broke, we immediately fell into the ranks, and began to ascend the hill. Motion is highly desirable to promote circulation and supple the joints after a rather cold night on the ground (as I frequently had an opportunity of remarking while in Mexico) and before we were half way up the hill I began to feel rather more comfortable. As we marched by a circuitous path, some of us turned occasionally to admire the appearance of the sky, which was tinted with a surpassing brilliance by the rising sun, while spread out beneath us, as far as the eye could reach, was some of the most picturesque and romantic scenery imaginable. But we were soon recalled to another sort of contemplation. A shot from the enemy's batteries, who had now caught a glimpse of us, followed by another and another in quick succession, soon dispelled any disposition to sentimentalize which we might have previously entertained. And having been cautioned to close up and quicken our steps, in a few minutes we gained the position we were to occupy, until the signal should be given for the charge.

There was a slight hollow in the top of the hill near where our twenty-four pounders were placed, and opposite Cerro Gordo; this was the position we ought to have maintained on the previous afternoon in place of following the Mexicans so rashly. In this hollow the rifles, a regiment of infantry, and our regiment, were ordered to lie down on the grass, in which position we were completely sheltered from the fire of the enemy's batteries. While lying thus, we could watch the effects of the grape shot passing a few feet above us, with its peculiar harsh and bitter whistle, to the opposite bank, where the saplings and branches crashed, under the withering influence of these unseen messengers, as if by magic. But soon our 24-pounders opened on the Mexicans with most terrible effect, as they were in a dense mass on the top of the opposite hill, where some thousands of infantry were crowded, to repel our anticipated assault. We now received orders to prepare for a charge. While the rifles were forming in the bottom of the hollow, one end of their line had incautiously gone a little way up on the opposite bank, or side of the hill. A shower of grape, that killed and wounded at least a dozen of their number, was the result of this exposure, and a volley of oaths from Colonel Harney, at the stupidity of the officer who had formed them in that position, seemed to grate as harshly on one's ears as the missiles showering over us.

While this was going on, a division of volunteers under General [Gideon J.] Pillow, had assaulted the batteries on our left, but were repulsed with considerable loss, General [James] Shields being amongst the severely wounded. The moment had now arrived when we were to face the horizontal shower which for the last hour and a half had been flying almost harmless over us. But the twenty-four pounders had done wonders, and Cerro Gordo was getting rather thinned of infantry by the panic created by their deadly discharges. The activity of the Mexican artillery was also rather slackened, they were evidently getting paralysed, and discouraged, at seeing the effects of our shots. Now was the time for the charge, and pausing for a few breathless moments till the next shower of grape hurtled over us, the bugle sounded the charge, and with a loud hurrah we leaped and tumbled down the ravine, opposite the enemy's battery of Ccrro Gordo.

A brisk fire of infantry opened upon us as we descended, and a few of our number dropped by the way; but we were in too great a hurry to stay and assist, or sympathize with wounded men just at that time. Bill Crawford, a Scotchman, and an old British soldier, with whom I had become acquainted at Vera Cruz, was going down the hill with me; we were within a few yards of each other, when recognising me he called out, "Ha! Geordie man, hoo are ye this morning, this is gey hot wark, how d'ye like this! Faith, Geordie; I doubt they've hit me," he continued, as he sat down behind a rock, a musket ball having entered the calf of his leg. I asked him if he was badly hurt. "I've gotten a scart that'll keep me frae gaun on; but gudesake, man, dinna mind me, I've shelter here; an I ken ye'll no like to be the last o' gaun up the hill." I had just jumped down four or five feet, when a rattle of grape that splintered a ledge of rock where I had stood while talking to Bill, showed me the danger of delay. "Ah, Geordie, a miss is as gude as a mile; gude bye, tak tent o' yoursel; tell our folk where I'm sitting, when it's ower," cried the hearty old fellow, who had come through the Peninsula and Waterloo, unhurt, to be wounded in this shabby affair, as I afterwards heard him express himself. It was not long before I reached the bottom of the hill.

On arriving there, both men and officers paused, but only for a few seconds, to recover breath. Here, feeling my havresac, containing biscuit and other articles, an incumbrance, I took it off and threw it down at the foot of a large rock, intending to call again for it if I could find an opportunity after the action.

We then began to climb the hill, which was very steep, but being rocky, and covered with brushwood for about two-thirds of the way, the enemy's musket balls passed quite harmlessly over us until near the top. When we arrived at the summit, a hundred or two of the Mexican infantry posted behind a breastwork of large stones, checked our advance for three or four minutes, until seeing us reinforced by a number of infantry coming up the hill cheering, they threw their muskets down, and scampered in the utmost confusion down the opposite side of the hill. Several of the enemy's guns were now manned, and fired on the retreating enemy, a disordered mass, running with panic speed down the hill, and along the road to Jalapa. The battle was now won; the other two forts, that a short time before had repulsed the volunteers, seeing the fate of Cerro Gordo, immediately pulled down their flag and hoisted a white one. They made an unconditional surrender, and the garrisons were marched out of the batteries to the road, without arms, to the amount of about 8000; they were employed to dig pits for the interment of the dead, and were afterwards permitted to go to their homes, on promising not to take up arms against the United States during the existing war.

* * *

General Scott was much censured by the men for releasing the prisoners taken at Cerro Gordo on the terms he did. It was argued that though he had no provisions, yet the road being open to Vera Cruz, a few hundred dragoons might have marched them back to that garrison, where supplies were plentiful, while the garrison left there would have been quite adequate to take charge of the prisoners. It certainly did seem rather questionable policy, as whatever were the faults of the Mexicans as soldiers, they were tolerable artillerists, and when inside one of their formidable batteries, the only position seemingly in which they would fight, they did us a good deal of damage before we succeeded in dislodging them. Now if he had kept these prisoners, it was evident that they would either have had to man their batteries with inferior men, in which case our army would have suffered less in the subsequent engagements; or wanting the assistance of those prisoners they might have been more inclined to come to terms. The letting them go, however, was not disapproved of by the Government, though among the soldiers of our regiment it was generally condemned when talking over the policy of the campaign.

We had now leisure to reflect upon our good fortune in having succeeded so much more easily than we anticipated in our hazardous assault, and I thought I perceived a moisture glistening in the eyes, and an unusual tremor affecting the voice of many brave soldiers, as they shook hands and congratulated each other on their mutual safety. Shortly afterwards General Scott with a few of his staff came riding up, and shaking hands with all who approached, congratulated them warmly on the victory. A number of the men and officers having crowded round him, he made a short and affecting speech, as near as I can recollect in the following words: — "Brother soldiers, I am proud to call you brothers, and your country will be proud to hear of your conduct this day. Our victory has cost us the lives of a number of brave men, but they died fighting for the honour of their country. Soldiers, you have a claim on my gratitude for your conduct this day, which I will never forget." During the delivery of this short address he was on horseback, and held his hat in his hand. He was very much affected, and tears rolled over the furrowed cheeks of the majestic old hero, the sight of which caused sympathetic drops to start to the eyes of many a rough and weather-beaten countenance, "albeit unused to the melting mood." At the conclusion, he was enthusiastically cheered, when he slowly rode off, bowing, and waving his hat.

Parties of the men were now despatched in all directions, to search for and bring in the wounded. A number of the men also set out in small parties to explore for water; as the morning being very hot, most of the men were suffering exceedingly from thirst. The wounded as they were brought in were attended to as well as under the circumstances could be expected, amputations being performed, and the most urgent and dangerous cases attended to first. One or two Mexican surgeons also made their appearance, and proceeded with much apparent skill to dress and bandage the wounds of their unfortunate countrymen, in which they were assisted by our surgeons, after they had dressed all their own wounded. These Mexican surgeons are reputed to be very skilful in the treatment of wounds, which seems likely enough; as there is probably no country in the world, if we except Texas, or California, where so large an amount of practice may be found in curing wounds of all the shooting and stabbing varieties. Be that as it may, however, it was currently reported that General Shields owed his life to the skill and care of a Mexican surgeon, who undertook and completed his cure after his wound had been pronounced mortal by those of our surgeons who examined it. Our wounded being supplied with blankets, and a sufficient number of men being appointed to attend on them, they were placed under a temporary shed which at least screened them from the scorching rays of the sun. Next day they were removed to Jalapa, where a large convent near the Plaza was appropriated to their use as a hospital.

In this engagement the American loss was between 500 and 600 in killed and wounded, and the Mexicans lost probably fully as many. Between 200 and 300 bodies of dead Mexicans were collected on the field, principally on the hill of Cerro Gordo, and a great many were killed by our dragoons and light artillery, who pursued them on the Jalapa road. Some of our men obtained considerable sums of money after the battle was over, by searching the clothes of the dead; but though the practice may be in accordance with the usages of war, there always seemed something so revolting to the feelings in it, that I could never think of trying that mode of recruiting my finances, though suffering a little sometimes from a deficiency of the exchequer. Neither was I the least singular in this respect, as I learned afterwards; the feeling being quite general amongst the men, more especially amongst the Irish, who had a superstitious horror at the idea of rifling a dead body, believing that it would be sure to call down a judgment on those who would do it, in a future engagement.

Several bodies of Mexican officers who had been killed while defending the hill, lay here, one of which was said to be that of a General who had been allowed to go on parole with the rest of the garrison from Vera Cruz when it capitulated. He was near the stockades, as if he had fallen while in advanced position, encouraging the soldiers by his example. One of our men had taken off his boots; the scoundrel, I am sure, would not be able to wear them, as the officer's feet, on which he had fine white stockings, were remarkably small. His hands too were very small and delicately formed, so much so as to cause remark by almost all who looked at the body. He was an old grey-headed man, seemingly about sixty years of age, of a rather slight though active make; and there was something noble in the expression of his countenance, which was calm and placid, as if he had died without pain. He was wounded with musket balls in two or three places of the body, and as he lay "with his face to the sky, and his feet to the foe," I could not help feeling a mingled thrill of admiration and pity at the fate of the brave old hero.

There was another Mexican officer breathing his last, near a small stone building which the Mexicans had used for a magazine, and on which they had a flag when we carried the hill. He was wounded in the breast with a musket-shot, and blood was oozing from his mouth. He was a large, stout-bodied man, and from the indications of Indian blood in his colour was evidently a Mexican, and not a pure Castilian like the other. A letter taken from his pocket contained his commission, dated only a few weeks before, and signed by Santa Anna, by which it appeared that he was Diego Martinez, *Capitan de Infanteria*. He wore a gold chain about his neck, to which was attached a miniature picture of a very fine-looking child; we could trace no resemblance in the child's countenance to his, but then his features were distorted by pain. Poor fellow, if many of the Mexican officers had imitated his example, I believe we should not have won the battle of Cerro Gordo so easily.

We now began to suffer from the cravings of hunger and thirst; few of the men had eaten anything that morning, in fact many of them had nothing to eat, and water could not be obtained even for the wounded, who felt a perpetual craving for it. I was therefore very glad when the adjutant coming up to where a group of us were standing, asked me if I thought I could find my way to where we had bivouacked on the previous night. It occurred to me that this would be a good chance to find some water; on my way I should also pass where I had left my havresac at the foot of the hill, and where Bill Crawford was wounded, and I should see whether he had been taken care of. I therefore told him I could find my way there easily. He then gave me a message to his servant, whom he had left behind with two horses in charge, his own and the colonel's, directing him to bring them round by the village, and wait with them at the bottom of the hill, as the regiment would march down in a short time. I started on my mission, and had little difficulty in finding my havresac; it lay in the position in which I had left it, nearly covered up with the long grass. I was very glad to see it, and picking it up I threw it over my shoulders, and pursued my journey. I soon came to the place where Crawford was wounded, but he was not there, so I was satisfied that he had been taken care of. I passed the dead bodies of a great many who had been killed the day before, both Americans and Mexicans, though principally the latter. They presented a shocking spectacle; these ghastly corpses but yesterday were as full of life and animation as I was at that moment, and now there they lay with their features distorted and blackening in the sun. I felt a sickening loathing at the idea of these human sacrifices, these offerings to Mars, which the poet and the historian dignify with the titles of glorious victories, and I cursed in my heart the infatuation which had linked me to the inhuman profession of a soldier.

I soon found the groom of the horses; he was an old grey-headed man, a countryman of mine, named David Gourley, and one of the finest old fellows in the regiment. After communicating my message, I got an invitation from him to take a little breakfast before starting, and I could have the adjutant's horse, he said, to ride to the bottom of the hill. I very gladly accepted both of these offers, feeling tired and faint; the excitement of the previous afternoon and that morning, with hunger and thirst, made me feel a strong inclination to lie down under a tree and enjoy a sound sleep. Observing my appearance of weariness, Gourley pulled out a flask from his havresac, which, having tasted, he handed to me, recommending it as a sovereign cure for lowness of spirits. I took a mouthful or two from the flask, which I found contained some excellent brandy, and felt immediate benefit from the invigorating cordial. "Ay, ay," said Gourley, as I handed it back to him, "ye'll come roun' bye and bye; Lord, man, ye glowred as if ye had seen a warlock a wee sin'; faith a mouthfu' o' that might be excused to a teetotaller on a morning like this. An' hoo did ye like ye'r race up the hill this morning, Geordie?" he continued; "faith, there's mony a braw fallow that'll never turn up a wee finger again, that got up this morning as well as you or I." I told him of several men who were killed and wounded whom he knew, and mentioned Billy Crawford. He said he had seen him; that he had got his leg dressed, and had been conveyed along with some others of the wounded to Plan del Rio. Having displayed his provisions, which consisted of some biscuit, and a few slices of fried beef, to which was added the luxury of a canteen of good water, I assisted my honest old friend to dispatch a most excellent breakfast, and having taken another mouthful of brandy, I felt like a new being.

*   *   *

Mounting the horses, we proceeded down the ravine to a small village on the road to Jalapa, and about a mile from Cerro Gordo. This was the place where Santa Anna had his headquarters for several days previous to the action. The Mexicans say he was the cause of their disgraceful conduct on that occasion; as he left precipitately an hour before the storming of Cerro Gordo, by his example so discouraging the officers and men — that they soon after broke and ran, believing the battle lost — when they heard that he had gone. It was commonly said and believed by our men, that in his hurry to be off he had left his wooden leg behind, and that it was preserved and sent home to the States as a trophy. As Santa Anna wears a *cork* leg, I think it is probable that the wooden leg found there must have belonged to some less illustrious personage. But the story was turned to good account by several enterprising Yankees, who for some months after continued to exhibit veritable wooden legs of "Santa Anna" through the towns and cities of the States, with great success, making a pretty considerable speculation of it. A more important prize consisted of several chests, or boxes, containing upwards of a hundred thousand silver dollars. One of the soldiers who first discovered it, had succeeded in breaking open one of the chests, and a few of the first comers had helped themselves to a pocketful, when an officer happened to arrive, who put a stop to further proceedings, by placing it under a secure guard, and reporting the seizure to General Scott.

On arriving at the village, we found it full of our infantry, our whole army nearly being drawn up in column, waiting the order to march. The Mexican troops having left their provisions behind, most of our men got some refreshment here, of which the poor fellows stood much in need. But a number of the small shops in the village having been supplied with aquadiente, for the purpose of retailing it to the soldiers of the Mexican army, there was a danger of our men getting drunk. To prevent this, the aquadiente was very properly ordered to be spilt, and I saw several barrels of it emptied upon the road, an officer standing by to see it effectually done. We also passed some companies where the officers were superintending the distribution of a portion of it, by seeing the sergeant serve the men with a glass of it in succession; this was a most judicious proceeding, which I am sure the men would appreciate. If officers were more generally aware what a large return of popularity they might secure among their men by ministering to the wants and comfort of those under their charge, I believe it would do much towards improving the condition of the army.

But in spite of every precaution, a number of the men I could see had got their canteens filled with the liquor, which had cost them nothing; all the houses in the village being robbed of their supplies of provisions and liquor in a very short time. A jolly fellow, belonging to an infantry regiment, came up to Gourley and me, and asked if we would drink the health of General Scott, handing us his canteen, which was full of aquadiente. We tasted his liquor, which was very fiery and unpalatable, when he very generously gave us a few *tortillas,* thin cakes made of Indian corn meal, and a piece of cheese, of which commodities he had a havresac nearly full. He advised us to dismount and have our canteens filled with the aquadiente, offering to show us where we could get it; but not wishing to quit our horses, for fear of losing them in the crowd, and the liquor, to judge from the specimen we had just tasted, not being very palatable, we declined his invitation.

After leaving the village, and as we passed on to the bottom of the hill of Cerro Gordo, we found the road strewed with the muskets and bayonets which the Mexicans had thrown away in their hasty retreat. These muskets were all of British manufacture, and had the *Tower* mark on their locks; but they were old and worn out, having evidently been condemned as unserviceable in the British army, and then sold to the Mexicans at a low price. Undoubtedly they were good enough for soldiers like the Mexicans, who generally throw them away on their retreat, but after examining a few of them I came to the conclusion that for efficient service one of our muskets was equal to at least three of them. Some thousands of these muskets were collected and destroyed, and the guns taken at the different forts were also burst and rendered unfit for use, by the men left behind for that purpose under the direction of an engineer officer. A great number of dead Mexicans, whose bodies had been collected for the purpose of interment, lay at the bottom of the hill. Among these we observed the body of a young and handsome though coarsely attired female, apparently not more than eighteen years of age. She had been the wife of one of the soldiers, and had stayed with him during the action. Perhaps they were newly married, and had been spending their honeymoon amid the horrid din of war. One could scarcely help wondering which among that group of ghastly corpses had been her husband. For among them he must be; it were impossible to picture him flying on the road to Jalapa, and leaving behind the bleeding corpse of his young and beautiful bride. The wives of the Mexican soldiers are in the habit of following the army, and sharing in the fatigues and dangers of a campaign, and there were several of them among the killed and wounded, both at this and at subsequent engagements. I was told of one woman who was wounded in the leg at this battle, who displayed a great deal of reluctance in allowing our surgeon to examine and dress the wound, though such extreme feelings of modesty, I am bound to acknowledge, are exceedingly rare among the women of the lower classes in Mexico.

Leaving Gourley at the bottom of the hill with the horses, I now proceeded to inform the adjutant that I had performed my mission. I found him seated on the ground, with Colonel Childs and several of the officers, and was proceeding to make my statement, when the colonel, interrupting me, exclaimed, "But where are the horses?" I told him I had got instructions from the adjutant to leave them at the bottom of the hill. The adjutant confirmed my statement, and appeared to think I had done very well; but still the colonel continued to mutter his dissatisfaction at my having obeyed the instructions too literally. I inwardly smiled at the unreasonable humour of the colonel, but at times like the present, when human life seems of about as much value as an old shoe, the humours of your big

men seem mere trivialities; and luckily for my equanimity, just
at that time, I felt a most sovereign contempt for the good or
bad opinion of breathing mortal, myself excepted. Besides
having satisfactorily obeyed my instructions, I had made an
excellent breakfast, and found my havresac. With these results
I felt very well satisfied; and if the colonel was not pleased,
why, he might whistle on his thumb.

About two or three o'clock our regiment was directed to
join the main body of the army, which had received orders to
proceed towards Jalapa. According to instructions, one company of our regiment was left to assist in the interment of the
dead, and the destruction of the guns and ammunition not considered requisite for the use of our own army. The regiment
then descended the hill of Cerro Gordo, and having taken its
place in the column, we were soon marching along the highway to Jalapa. A great quantity of clothing abandoned by the
Mexicans strewed the road, and as many of our men had
neither great-coat nor blanket, having left them in the baggage
waggons at Plan del Rio, they eagerly appropriated those which
the Mexicans had thrown away. But they soon discovered that
they had made a most miserable prize, few or none of these
clothes being wholly free from a tormenting and disgusting
species of vermin to which the Mexicans seem universally accustomed and reconciled. Most of the men, on discovering the
condition of these clothes, threw them away, but a number
retained possession of some of them; and from that period until
after we entered the city of Mexico, even those most scrupu-
lously attentive to personal cleanliness could not wholly divest
themselves from that most annoying and detestable of the
plagues of Egypt. After entering the city, we were supplied
with new clothing, and being in tolerable quarters, and furnished with a plentiful supply of soap and clean water, we
succeeded after a time in eradicating the abominable pest. We
only marched about eight miles that evening, bivouacking on
the grass plats that stretched along each side of the road. A
small stream of clear water which the Mexicans had conducted

a distance of ten miles, by cutting a channel for it along the edge of the road, to supply the garrison at Cerro Gordo, supplied our evening beverage, and as we were tired with the excitement and fatigues of the day, we were soon folded in the arms of Morpheus.

* * *

Roused from our sound slumbers by the bugle at daybreak next morning, we were soon on our march again for Jalapa. After marching a few miles we came to Encerro, the favourite residence of Santa Anna, who owns a large and fertile tract in that neighbourhood. The house in which he had formerly lived — called by our men *Santa Anna's House* — is a large plain building on the side of a hill, about a mile from the road, and on the left hand going to Jalapa. Its situation is admirable, the view of the surrounding country being of the most delightful character, wooded mountains and grassy plain stretching away as far as the eye can reach. But water, that principal auxiliary to fine landscape scenery, it lacks in common with most Mexican scenery. True, a rivulet crosses the highway at Encerro about the size of a Scotch burn, which leaps and tumbles in a series of sparkling cascades down a romantic and deep rocky glen on the right hand; but any rivulet or sheet of water large enough to give a tone to the extended landscape, one may look for in vain in that portion of the country that lies between Vera Cruz and the city of Mexico.

We experienced no interruption from the Mexicans on our march; indeed it would have been strange if we had, considering their contemptible defence of Cerro Gordo.

These mesons are so nearly alike in their accommodations for travellers in all the towns and villages on the road from Vera Cruz to the city of Mexico, with the exceptions of Jalapa and Puebla, that one description may suffice for all. They are usually built in the form of a large square, the buildings being one story high. The front of the square, through the centre of which there is a wide entrance, carefully closed at night by a large gate, contains the domestic establishment of the proprietor, with his offices and kitchens. The furthest end of the square is a range of sheds furnished with stalls and feeding troughs for an unlimited number of quadrupeds, and the sides of the square are ranges of small unventilated apartments, about six feet by ten, with a door in the centre, but no windows. Into one of these cells the traveller and his luggage are stowed; he makes his bed, if he is so fortunate as to possess the means of doing so, on the floor, never very clean, but which he may sweep if he can find a broom on the premises. An air of the most perfect contempt for the virtue of cleanliness pervades every corner of the establishment, and the bill of fare is usually limited to a very few simple dishes, among which *tortillas* and *frijoles*, maize cakes, and beans stewed in lard, form prominent items. In short, the person purposing to visit Mexico who is not prepared for being robbed on the highway by banditti, or is nice in the article of diet, or not impervious to the attacks of fleas and other unmentionable vermin, would be wise either to lay up a considerable share of stoical endurance, and resolve to submit heroically to the force of circumstances, or altogether abandon the rash purpose.

We remained in Tepe Agualco two days, as General [George] Cadwallader wished to allow a reinforcement of troops under General Pierce, who were only two or three days' march in rear of us, to come up with our division. Pulque is one of the principal products of Tepe Agualco, and three or four old women were seated in front of one of the mesons, each with a pitcher of that liquor and an earthen jug, which held nearly a pint, and which they sold for *dos clacos*, about three cents. I drank a jug full of it, and although the first time I had tasted it, relished it very much. It produced the same sort of exhilarating effect as an equal quantity of moderately strong ale.

On the 1st of July we commenced our march over an extensive plain, uncultivated, except an occasional patch of beans or barley along the edge, at the bottom of mountains which bound it. The plains here are covered with short grass, and a variety of flowering and sweet-scented herbs, and in the morning when we began our march the air was deliciously perfumed with the odour they diffused as we trod on them. In the neighbourhood of Tepe Agualco the plain is covered with pumice stones. These some inventive genius conceived the idea of converting into tobacco pipes, by cutting the soft stone into the shape of a bowl, and sticking a reed or hollow tube into it. Our supply of pipes had become quite exhausted, and none could be procured, as the Mexicans never use anything but the *cigarito* or *puro* in smoking. Necessity suggested the pumice stone, which answered the purpose so well that one-half of the men might be seen smoking them in the course of a day or two after the first one had been seen. I may remark for the benefit of the reader that a *puro* means a cigar, and a *cigarito* is only a small quantity of finely-cut tobacco rolled up in a paper about a couple of inches long, and the thickness of a very fine quill. One puro or cigar contains as much tobacco and will cost as much money as twenty cigaritos. You may have a bundle of cigaritos containing from fifty to a hundred for *une medio* (six cents), but you can only purchase about two or three puros for the same sum.

The plains, or table lands, *tierra templada*, commence a few miles from Perote, and this *plateau* continues to a considerable distance beyond Puebla, where a high range of mountains divides it from the valley of Mexico. These plains, which are perfectly level, and on which there is not a single tree, ditch, fence, or habitation, or a shrub higher than a man's knee, present a desolate and deserted appearance. They are everywhere bounded by mountains, and vary in width from thirty or forty to eight or ten miles, where they are narrowed by the spurs of opposite mountain ranges. The villages or haciendas are built in retired nooks behind the skirt of the hills which bound them, and any partial cultivation visible from Perote to Nopaluco, a distance of between forty and fifty miles, is a slight patch at the foot of the mountains. There are a few exceptions to this general description, and round Perote, Nopaluco, Amazook, Puebla, and San Martin, there are portions of the soil tolerably well cultivated. But these cover a small portion of the *tierra templada,* and I think there is not a twentieth part of the available surface of the country under cultivation between Vera Cruz and the city of Mexico that would be in a short period if the country was possessed by a more active and vigorous race. After a march of about fifteen miles we arrived and encamped at a place called *Ojo de Agua* (the Eye of Water); a spring which gushes out from a rock in the side of a hill here gives the name to the place. It is a shallow, insignificant stream at its source, but it gradually widens, and about a quarter of a mile from the spring my comrade Nutt and I found it wide enough to bathe in.

On the fifth and sixth we remained in the vicinity of *Ojo de Agua* to enable General [Franklin] Pierce's division to overtake ours before we undertook to pass the Pinol, a dangerous pass, about eighteen or twenty miles further on. On the morning of the seventh we again resumed our march, and about ten o'clock we arrived at Nopaluco, where we halted to procure water and such refreshments as the place afforded. A quantity of fruit and other edibles speedily made their appearance in the market, and I breakfasted luxuriously on fresh bread, delicious ripe bananas, and chocolate, for *une real,* (twelve and a half cents). Nopaluco is built of adobe or unburnt brick, and is finely situated on a gentle rise. The land for several miles round is tolerably well cultivated in wheat, barley, Indian corn, and the agave. About three o'clock we reached the edge of the pass, where we encamped for the night.

On the morning of the eighth, General Pierce's division joined, having been encamped a short distance behind ours on the previous night. A strong body of skirmishers were sent up to explore the woods, crowning the precipitous cliffs which overhung our road for several miles, and on the edge of which cliffs the enemy had poised huge masses of rock ready to tumble on our approach, but no trace of an enemy could be discovered. After all their preparations they had very prudently given up the attempt, and we passed the Pinol without hearing a shot fired. After leaving this pass, our road for a few miles passed over what seemed the bed of a mountain torrent, it was so torn up and furrowed by the heavy rains; a considerable tract of loose sand, interspersed with large masses of porphyry, succeeded, until we arrived near Amazook, where the country is very well cultivated. Like all the small Mexican towns on this road, Amazook consists of a collection of adobe and mud buildings, with the exception of a few of the principal houses in the Plaza, where there is also a very handsome church. The principal feature in every little town and village in Mexico is the church. It is always quaint-looking and picturesque, and invariably beside the Plaza. It is not customary to have the burial-grounds adjacent to the churches in Mexico. In spite of the dirt, slovenliness, and misery which seem to envelope the population and their wretched-looking habitations, the towns and villages of Mexico have always a remarkably picturesque appearance. I believe a good deal of this effect is produced by the remarkable purity of the atmosphere, and their quaint old churches, with their exterior carved and painted decorations. The Plaza, being the market-place, is usually a large open space, giving effect to the view of the church, and it mostly contains a fountain of water in its centre, and has a row of trees around it, which also adds to the general effect.

On the ninth we marched through a tolerably well-cultivated tract of country to Puebla. As we approached within five or six miles of the city we enjoyed one of the finest views of a city at a distance that I have ever seen. The lofty snow mountains of Popocatepetl and Iztaccihuatl, with their broad and heavy-looking dark bases, and their dazzlingly bright pyramidal summits, rose in the background. In front, on the side of a gently rising and delightfully wooded hill, sat Puebla, every outline of its numerous spires and churches seen through the highly-rarified and transparent atmosphere as distinctly as the lines of a highly-finished engraving. On arriving at Puebla our company, on account of requiring accommodation for the horses, were comfortably quartered in a large *meson,* where we remained until the army marched on the capital.

* * *

Puebla is distant from the city of Mexico 93 miles, and from Vera Cruz 186 miles; the distance from Vera Cruz to the city of Mexico by the road being 279 miles, though in a direct line, I believe, it is not more than 150. The Spaniards have a proverb, "Puebla the first heaven, Mexico the second," and I believe there can be no question as to the superiority of the site on which Puebla is built as regards its salubrity and healthiness. The situation of Puebla does credit to the taste and judgment of the Spaniards; this being one of the few cities founded by them in Mexico, the others being principally on the foundations of Indian towns and cities. It is built on the side of a beautifully wooded hill, and its streets, though not very wide, are well paved, and have good side walks of flagstone. The houses are mostly two stories high, some of them being gaudily, some fantastically, and others tastefully, ornamented with painting and carving. Many of them have the entire front inlaid with painted and glazed tiles, and the whole produces a sort of bizarre, yet rich and pleasing effect. One of the suburbs contains a fine public garden called the *Alameda;* it is more than a mile in circumference, adorned with fountains, *jets d'eaux,* and statues, and is very neatly kept in order, and tastefully ornamented with flowering shrubs and trees. The houses are all built of stone, and large and commodious, and but a small portion of their number would seem to denote poverty; yet the city swarms with squalid beggars, clothed in rags and exposing their diseases and deformities. There are several cotton factories in operation in Puebla when things are in a peaceable state, and a number of Englishmen are employed in them at high wages, superintending and instructing the natives there employed. But the war had stopped all the machinery, and some thousands of the inhabitants of Puebla, thrown out of employment, were suffering great privation, both from that circumstance and the rise in the price of commodities, caused by the presence of such a large body of our army. The goods made in Puebla are very dear, and of coarse qualities, and only for the enormous duties levied on foreign goods, these cotton factories could not be carried on at all. The new tariff by which American goods were admitted at an almost nominal duty, had caused the stoppage of all the manufacturing machinery in Mexico.

There are said to be more than a hundred domes and spires in this city, which has a population of 80,000. It abounds in convents, and each of these distributes daily an allowance of provisions at the convent door, without money and without price, or even the formality of a ticket from a member of the mendicity society; a discriminating charity being no part of the policy of the Church of Rome, one of whose deliberate aims seems to be the fostering of ignorance and poverty. To endeavour to unfetter agricultural, manufacturing, and commercial industry, and to have the accursed laws of peonage abolished, so that the people might gradually emerge from this miserable serfdom to a more elevated and self-dependent state, would scarcely suit the views of that Church. I believe the jealous system of Spain in discouraging commerce and free intercourse between her possessions and those of other countries, was dictated by the Church of Rome, afraid of the dangerous activity of mind which commerce and manufactures must inevitably produce. Every stranger who visits Mexico, and does not wilfully shut his eyes to the fact, must perceive the culpability of the clergy in causing and perpetuating the present condition of affairs. They seem to have cared about nothing but the endowment of churches, ornamenting of shrines, and all the childish mummery of their pageantry. Under the present system of religious intolerance which prevails in Mexico, it cannot be expected that the country will become progressive or prosperous. And if anything can reconcile one to the injustice of carrying the war into the interior of Mexico, it would be the benefit that might possibly result, by showing the Mexicans the grievous inferiority of vigorous action which the deadening influence of this system has produced.

The convents and public buildings in Puebla afforded ample accommodation to our army, but few of our men seemed to enjoy robust health. The sick list and the hospitals were full to overcrowding, and one-half of those doing duty, wasted with diarrhoea, looked like skeletons or mummies; the hardships and privations of the previous part of the campaign, telling more or less severely on nearly all, and one could not walk far through the streets of Puebla without hearing the mournful strains of the soldier's funeral procession. At Perote too, where a large number of sick had been left, the castle having been converted into a depôt, the sick died at the average rate of twelve a-day for a series of months. These were interred without any military formalities, or even the usual burial service, being wrapped in the blankets in which they died, they were carted out and thrown into pits dug for the purpose daily outside of the garrison. I suffered a good deal for several months with the prevalent complaint, but like a great many others continued to do duty when not very able, being determined not to give in if possible. I derived considerable benefit from the use of pulque and aquadiente, and at other times from opium, a small piece of which I carried in a box in my pocket during the campaign, frequently taking a few grains of it before going to sleep at night.

The rainy season was now nearly over, and all attempts at negotiation with the enemy, who it was now known had fortified the approaches to the capital, having failed, General Scott being ready for the field about the beginning of August, decided on moving towards the city of Mexico. Accordingly on the 6th of August the first division marched under the command of General Worth, on the 8th, the second division under the command of General Twiggs, and the third under General

Pillow on the 9th. The company to which I belonged had turned in the two 12-pounders which we brought up from Jalapa, and had got instead a light battery consisting of two 6-pounder field pieces, and two 12-pounder howitzers. We now belonged to General Pillow's division. The whole effective strength of our army, which was subdivided into three nearly equal divisions, consisted of about ten thousand men, including cavalry and artillery. Of cavalry, we had about a thousand, three troops of light artillery, one heavy field battery, and a siege train consisting of a few large mortars and guns.

On the morning of the 9th of August, on leaving Puebla, we passed through a partially cultivated tract for a considerable distance. About six miles from Puebla we passed, two or three miles off, on the left side of the road, the ruins of Cholula, an Indian city, which the Spaniards destroyed on taking possession of the country. A pyramid erected before the arrival of Cortez is still standing, and we could see it distinctly from the road. It was covered with shrubs, and presented the appearance of a natural hill, with a neat church on the top of it. Its height is said to be a hundred and sixty-two feet, and each side of its base 1300 feet. It is built of unburnt bricks and clay, and contains cavities intended for sepulchres. There are about 6000 inhabitants in Cholula, and they still manufacture a description of earthenware for which they were famous in the time of Cortez. We met some of these Indians carrying immense loads of this earthenware to Puebla for sale. It is surprising what heavy loads they carry on their backs for a long distance to market. I have frequently seen them bringing a load weighing at least a hundred pounds to the city of Mexico, which I was assured they had brought on their backs from the mountain eight or ten miles off. They support the burden behind by a strap which passes across their forehead, and carry a stick with which they prop it when they are tired.

We encamped about twelve miles from Puebla on a meadow by the roadside, where there was a pond of indifferent water.

But San Martin was twelve miles further and there was no other place nearer, and as the next stage between San Martin and Rio Frio was twenty-four miles, and difficult for the horses, being mostly up hill, it was necessary they should be fresh for that day's march. San Martin, which we made our second day's stage, is a small town containing a church and convent, and surrounded by a tract of fertile and well-cultivated land. We left San Martin early on the morning of the third day's march, and after passing through a tract of country covered with loose stones of porphyry, and sprinkled with pines and cedars, began to ascend the hills that separate the valley of Puebla from that of Mexico. After marching about the half of our day's journey we arrived at a well-built stone bridge thrown over a deep precipitous gorge, with a stream of good water in a rocky channel at the bottom. A little way up the hill on the other side of the bridge, we halted at a *meson*, and here my comrade Bill Nutt and myself, with several other fortunate individuals, were in time to procure some fresh bread, sausages, and a drop of *aquadiente*. Our road for the remainder of the day's march was up hill, rough, and through a thick wood of pines. After travelling up hill for two or three hours, we began to descend into the valley of the *Rio Frio* (Cold River). The enemy we could see had made some preparations for defending the pass by forming breastworks of felled trees at various parts of it; but they had afterwards abandoned the idea, being resolved, we supposed, to concentrate their forces in defending the near approaches to the city. Descending into the valley we passed *Rio Frio*, an insignificant stream, which runs across the road, and which deserves its name, as it is nearly as cold as ice. It comes down from the snow mountains and is shaded from the hot rays of the sun by the fine woods through which it passes. We encamped on a fine grassy plain a little beyond it. We began our march early next morning, and kept winding round hills covered with thick woods of pines, and carpeted with a variety of wild flowers, until about eleven o'clock, when we reached a meson on the summit of the mountain, and obtained a view of the far-famed valley of Mexico.

Description is tame when one tries to convey the impression which this scene usually makes on all who see it for the first time. It is certainly the most magnificent view in Mexico; perhaps, of the peculiar description, the first in the world. At an elevation of about 3000 feet, the spectator sees, as if spread at his feet like a map, the whole of the valley of Mexico, its circumference, at the base of the mountains which form the sides of the mighty basin, being 120 miles, and at the crest of the mountain 200 miles. The whole of the plain, from the height on which the spectator stands, is distinctly taken in at one view, and the most minute details are distinctly defined and delineated, owing to the remarkable transparency and purity of the atmosphere. The towers and spires of the city of Mexico, twenty-five miles distant, are distinctly seen peering out from the foliage and trees; almost the only part of the valley where trees are to be seen, by the by, is that round the city. The remainder of the valley presents the uniform appearance of a large green plain, dotted with white churches, spires, and haciendas, and containing several large sheets of water, the remains of the lakes which are said to have once nearly covered the whole valley. Several small insulated mountains may also be distinctly discerned, the only large objects that rise on the surface of the vast unbroken green plain. The mountains of Popocatepetl and Iztaccihuatl, its brother giant, rise about twenty miles to the left, and tower to a height of 7000 feet higher than where the spectator is standing, though owing to the bright atmosphere and the sun shining on the snow, it seems only two or three miles distant. The whole of this beautiful valley is hemmed in by a circle of stupendous, rugged and dark mountains, the rough but sublime setting of nature to one of her most inimitable pictures, and forming a most perfect combination of the sublime and beautiful.

Seen from that elevation, the valley of Mexico is a most glorious and magnificent sight, but " 'tis distance lends enchantment to the view," and we descend into it, its beauties vanish. The lakes become marshes, the fields are not cultivated, the villages are mud, and the inhabitants wretched-looking Indian peons, in rags and squalid misery. We encamped outside of a small town, called Chalco, on the lake of that name, and near the left edge of the valley. On descending the hill, where we lay two days, General Scott in the meantime having reconnoitred the enemy's fortifications at the Peñon, decided on trying if another way could not be found to reach the city. Colonel Duncan having satisfied General Scott that a road for artillery could be cut from Chalco to Augustine, General North's division moved in that direction on the 15th, followed by Twiggs's and Pillow's. We marched by short day's stages over a terribly bad road, and on the 18th we arrived at Augustine, within a few miles of the enemy's position.

*   *   *

On arriving at San Augustine we encamped in the main *plaza*, stretching our picket ropes across the trees that surrounded it, to which we fastened our horses by the halters, but without taking off their harness until further orders. A large force of the enemy had left San Augustine shortly before we arrived; they had some intention of making a stand, and opposing our entrance to the village, it was said, but their courage had gradually oozed out as we approached over the adjacent plain. San Augustine is a neat little town, with a fine old church, and a large *plaza* well ornamented and shaded with trees. But it had a very deserted appearance, most of the inhabitants having left in consequence of the anticipated battle to be fought there, or in the vicinity. Only a few had stayed in charge of goods and such property as they had been unable to remove easily. This was the first place in which I had seen apples since I came to Mexico, several Indian women being here with baskets of them, ripe, mellow, and delicious. As these poor people eagerly exchanged them for biscuits, a rapid transfer of the contents of the soldiers' havresacs and their baskets speedily took place, to the mutual satisfaction of the parties. I ate a couple of them, and I do not think I ever relished an apple so much before or since, which is not much to be wondered at considering the heat and thirst of the few days' march preceding. These apples were very abundant in the neighbourhood of San Augustine, where I saw some of the finest orchards I have ever seen; our men suffering a good deal from heat and thirst, were sometimes tempted to indulge in them to an injurious excess. Indeed our surgeons generally blamed the excessive use of fruit as a principal cause of the mortality of the troops during the whole campaign.

After the return of a party who had been reconnoitring the enemy's position, and found them strongly entrenched on the side of a hill commanding the road to Mexico, we received orders to take up our quarters for the night but to hold ourselves in readiness for a sudden call, being cautioned against leaving the camp. General Scott wished to know as accurately as possible the strength of the enemy's position, before hazarding an engagement, a desire to gain a victory with the smallest possible sacrifice of life, being a decided characteristic of that excellent commander, who knew that however despicable an enemy may be in the field, he may become formidable if unwisely attacked while strongly entrenched and fortified, and occupying an advantageous position. Our infantry were quartered in the various empty buildings in the town which had been deserted by their owners, while our captain decided that our company should pitch their tents in the *plaza*, and remain there with our battery. Our horses were put up, however, in an empty range of stables at one end of the *plaza*, being still left in harness in case of a sudden call for their services. A guard of twelve men and a corporal having been ordered by the captain, I found that it was my turn to mount that evening. Having according to instructions posted four sentries, one on the officers' quarters, one on the horses, and two on the guns and ammunition in the *plaza*, I marched the remainder of the guard to the stable-yard, where, finding a butcher's shop and dwelling-house empty, but locked-up, we very deliberately forced the lock, and appropriated the building to the use of the guard. This proceeding of ours was strictly in order; but even if it had been rather irregular, the exigencies of the case might almost warrant our proceedings. It had begun to rain, and the nights at that season and in that high region are excessively cold, and unless we had secured a building of some sort for the use of our guard, we should have suffered from cold and wet during the whole night. During all that day until near evening we expected an immediate engagement, there being a constant cannonading interchanged between the enemy's entrenchments and our heavy field battery. This firing we learned was in consequence of a reconnoitring party, consisting of several engineer officers, having been observed by the enemy, who opened a fire on the party, killing Captain Thornton of the dragoons, and seriously injuring a guide. In the evening, the firing having ceased, strong out-lying piquets were stationed outside of the town of San Augustine, and we were told to be ready for an attack on the enemy's position next day.

In the meantime we made ourselves very comfortable in our guard-house, having kindled a large fire and procured an ample supply of wood to last during the night. The butcher had left a quantity of sheep skins, which were perfectly dry, and had the wool on; these being laid on benches, or even on the floor, formed a most luxurious couch; though certainly to a person of the most delicate olfactory nerves, I believe they would have seemed rather redolent of a peculiar odorous effluvium, exceedingly suggestive of dead mutton. But that was a trifle compared with the grateful softness and warmth derived from lying on them; we were, therefore, very well contented with our quarters for the night. The fact of the matter is, that in our present circumstances small favours were generally very thankfully accepted; cold, hunger, thirst, mental anxiety, and bodily suffering, being admirable cures for fastidiousness. The rose leaf frets the Sybarite, while a bundle of straw is a luxury to a beggar, or a parcel of rank-smelling sheepskins to a poor, tired and half-starved soldier upon a campaign. Having found a large copper boiler on the premises, such as the Mexican butchers use to melt lard in, some one suggested that as we had a good fire we might have a supper cooked in it for the whole guard. This was a very good idea; and a few active foragers were immediately despatched on a secret expedition for the purpose of levying contributions wherever they could be most easily collected. These were successful beyond expectation, speedily returning with supplies which gave us anticipations of a feast such as we had not beheld, except in dreams, for a long time previously. After an inspection of the stock of provisions on hand, with the very handsome additions made by our active and highly-intelligent party of foragers, for which they received high commendations, the dish which seemed best adapted to our circumstances, and which we agreed to have cooked, was a sort of gipsy hodge-podge or Salmagundi; in fact a heterogeneous omnigatherum of all come-at-able comestibles. In the first place, we had a quantity of biscuit, the proceeds of the joint contributions of our havresacs, several pounds of bacon furnished by Government, having been procured without leave asked or obtained, from one of the wagons containing supplies for Uncle Sam's troops; and further by supplies obtained by our party of foragers, one turkey, two fowls, a piece of mutton, some potatoes, chili peppers, tomatoes, and onions. These various ingredients being first well cleaned, were cut into pieces, and the whole compound being seasoned with salt and pepper, was afterwards boiled in the huge cauldron, which was propped in the centre of the floor by three stones, for the purpose of admitting the fire under it. After our potage had been sufficiently boiled, we resolved on inviting a few of our comrades to the feast, as it was evident that there would be at least twice as much as we could consume, and it would be a pity that any of our delicious fare should be lost. Accordingly every one bringing a comrade, we soon had an addition of ten or twelve more to our party, forming, about ten o'clock on the same night, a snug little party of about twenty.

Everything went off admirably, as the phrase is. The dish or the mode of cooking it was not perhaps the most scientific, yet I am persuaded from the celerity with which it disappeared, and the apparent gusto that marked the process, that it was relished as highly and gave as much satisfaction as if it had been the most elaborate specimen of artistic cookery ever served up at the table of the most aristocratic of the clubs of London. The hilarity of the evening was wonderfully augmented by the addition to our company of those comrades who had been invited; for several of them, having found their way into a liquor store in the evening, had filled their canteens with *mezcal*, a coarse and not very palatable spirituous liquor, but highly stimulating and intoxicating, and therefore nectar to a soldier on occasions like the present. This liquor which they had brought with them, they now produced as their quota to the feast. To drink ardent spirits when upon guard is strictly forbidden by the rules of the service, but the absurd strictness of the prohibition renders it completely null. I must say that in the whole course of my experience I never knew or heard of a soldier refusing a glass of spirits while on guard, on the ground of its being an infringement of military discipline. Paradoxical as it may seem, I believe that the utmost latitude permitted to the soldier in some of these matters, would, by producing habits of self-control, act as a far better preventive to the crime of drunkenness than the present system. Unless a soldier acquires the habit of self-control as regards the use or abuse of ardent spirits (and no person has greater need to do so), prohibitions and threats of punishment are rather worse than useless — they are mischievous: but if he has acquired these habits, these prohibitions are not needed.

On the present occasion, however, I felt that there was no danger of any of the present company rendering themselves unfit for duty, as we were all well aware that we had work before us next day, for which a night's debauch would be a sorry preparation. I have observed that men, careless of consequences on other occasions, are cautious of allowing themselves to become intoxicated before an expected engagement. This caution on the part of the soldier probably arises from a dread of the imputation of cowardice, and a fear of losing caste among his comrades, by making it seem as if he was seeking to supply a deficiency of native stamina and nerve, through the medium of a foreign and artificial stimulus and excitement. In some cases also it may be the result of a knowledge of the dangers of too free indulgence at a time when all require the perfect use of their faculties for the performance of their duties. Soldiers are mostly keenly sensitive to the ridicule of their companions, whose good opinion they generally esteem more highly than that of their officers. To stand well in the estimation of his special comrades, and of the company to which he belongs, is the most powerful incentive to the soldier's good conduct in the field of action; and in the absence of a brave officer to lead them to the attack, the love of Bill, Tom, or Harry's approbation, or the dread of being called a coward, has often been the means of gaining the battle.

... To return to our convivial party in the guard-house, songs and toasts began to circulate with the aquadiente, while the expected battle of next day engrossed a considerable share of the conversation. "Come, my lads," said Corporal Bell, a north of Ireland man, who spoke in a broad Scotch dialect, "here's a toast — May the balls be divided to-morrow, the same as the pay and the honour." "Bravo! Corporal Bell's song — a song from Corporal Bell, 'Bucking and Gagging,' " * shouted a dozen voices at once. "I say, boys," expostulated a sentry, looking in, "you had better not make just so much noise if you don't want the officer of the day here." "Ay, faith, freen, ye're no far wrong," said Corporal Bell, while handing him the canteen; "here, man, take a drap o' that to keep the could frae ye'r stomach. I say, lads," he continued, addressing the party, "we

---

* A favourite mode of punishment in the American service.

had better ca' canny, or faith, we'll maybe hae some bucking and gagging instead o' singing aboot it." "Is it the night before a fight," cries Mike Ryan; "by the holy fist of the blessed Saint Patrick, the mean schaming villains, that are so ready to ill use a poor devil at other times, are mighty kind an' civil them days. The devil a taste o' fear of any bucking an' gagging for this night any way; so, if you plase, Corporal Bell, just favour the present company with a few verses." "Weel, lads, I'll just sing you a verse or twa aboot bucking an' gagging, an' then we maun toddle awa' an' tak' a bit sleep, an' be ready for our work in the morning." So saying he commenced, in a good sonorous but subdued voice, to sing the following verses: —

Come, all Yankee soldiers, give ear to my song,
It is a short ditty, 'twill not keep you long;
It's of no use to fret on account of our luck,
We can laugh, drink, and sing yet in spite of the buck.
                              Derry down, &c.

"Sergeant, buck him, and gag him," our officers cry,
For each trifling offence which they happen to spy;
Till with bucking and gagging of Dick, Tom, and Bill,
Faith, the Mexican ranks they have helped to fill.
                              Derry down, &c.

The treatment they give us, as all of us know,
Is bucking and gagging for whipping the foe;
They buck us and gag us for malice or spite,
But they're glad to release us when going to fight.
                              Derry down, &c.

A poor soldier's tied up in the sun or the rain,
With a gag in his mouth till he's tortured with pain;
Why I'm bless'd, if the eagle we wear on our flag,
In its claws shouldn't carry a buck and a gag.
                              Derry down, &c.

"What the devil is that?" cried several voices at once, as a loud rumbling noise resembling thunder, was heard. On opening the guard-room door the cause was soon apparent. The place where we had stabled our horses was an old rickety shed, with a shingle roof supported by three rows of wooden posts, one on each side of the shed and one in the centre. Running along the centre of the shed, there was a long wooden trough to which our horses were fastened by the halters; several of the horses had been fastened to the posts also, which being rotten had given way, and a large portion of the roof having fallen in on the top of the horses, they were kicking up a complete rumpus. A sentry, who was over the horses, was also jammed in among them, and we were afraid he would be injured. Cautioning him to remain quiet a little until we got a light, we speedily procured a lanthorn, and succeeded in extricating him safely, and also in unfastening and leading out the most entangled among the horses. Still as it was necessary to remove all the horses to some other place, it being evident that the remainder of the shed would be pulled down if it were not speedily done, I thought best to acquaint the officer of the day. I, therefore, sent one of the guard to his quarters to tell him the condition of the shed, and to ask for instructions as to where the horses should be taken to. The officer sent word back to have the whole company roused and turned out, and that he would be over presently himself. Accordingly in a few minutes he arrived, and having given directions to stretch the picket rope in the *plaza*, and lead the horses out and fasten them to it, in less than half-an-hour everything was right again. On examining the horses, several of them were found to have received slight injuries, but nothing to render them unfit for duty next day. Our party having been thus suddenly dissolved did not assemble again, and desirous of recruiting my strength for the next day, I lay down to sleep.

* * *

Next morning about 5 o'clock we were roused by the reveille bugle, and having fed our horses and taken breakfast, we were ordered to harness the horses, and hitch them in the carriages. Regiments of infantry continued to arrive and form in the Plaza until it and the adjacent streets were crowded, and between 7 and 8 o'clock our force consisting of about five thousand infantry, two light batteries, and a squadron of dragoons, began the march for Contreras. The ground occupied by the enemy had been well reconnoitred on the previous day; they were entrenched on the side of a hill on the left hand side of the road leading to the city where they had thrown up embankments of earth, and had a strong battery of very heavy guns. As it was evident that to go by the main road would expose us to the fire of this battery, which we had no means of returning with effect, General Scott had decided on approaching their position by a circuitous route. We therefore commenced our march down a country road, leading through orchards and cornfields, while a great deal of caution was used in advancing, the division being halted every few minutes and skirmishers sent out in front and on the flanks. At last after ascending a steep hill where we had some difficulty with our battery, having to get a regiment of infantry with drag ropes to assist us in bringing up our guns and caissons, we came in sight of the enemy. We halted within two or three miles of them, while General Scott and his staff ascended a hill on our right for the purpose of obtaining a good view of their position. After resting about ten minutes we received the order to move on to the attack. The Rifles and another infantry regiment, were directed to drive in a body of skirmishers occupying a cornfield about a mile and a half in front of the enemy's position, and between us and them. Our battery was to go on at the same time, and take up a position where it could annoy the enemy. When we came to the edge of the cornfield, to admit our battery we had to pull down a piece of wall built of large pieces of lava piled on one another in the manner in which they build dry stone walls, or what are called in Scotland *dry stane dykes*. While we were busily engaged in pulling down the wall, which took us a few minutes, as the heavy masses of lava required several men to roll them one by one out of the way, the enemy commenced throwing large shells, a few of

which dropped very near, but fortunately without doing us
any injury. In the mean time General Twiggs, who, being in
rear a little, did not perceive the cause of this delay, rode up,
calling out, "Captain [John B.] Magruder, why don't you go
forward with the battery?" "So I will, general, as soon as my
men can remove a piece of the wall which our battery is surely
not expected to clear at a flying leap," was the reply of the
captain. "Well, where are the rifles?" the general asked, "why
don't they drive in those Mexican vagabonds; forward with
the rifles; forward with the rifles; we must either make a spoon
or spoil a horn this day." "Faith I doot some o' us 'll no hae
muckle mair use for a spoon after this day's wark's ower," drily
remarked a Scotchman belonging to the rifles, who was helping
to clear the way for our battery. The rifles, and the other infantry regiment, scrambled over the wall as our battery began
to move, and were soon busily engaged with the enemy, whose
balls came whistling among us, wounding two of our riders,
who had to fall to the rear.

The field or plain over which we were advancing is strewed
with large masses of lava. Between these we had to thread our
way with the guns and caissons, sometimes brought to an
abrupt halt by a mass of stubborn rock, over which we had to
lift the carriages as if over a wall, the men lifting at the wheels
and the horses whipped to their utmost exertions at the same
time. At last after a great deal of exhausting fatigue we succeeded in planting our battery in front of the enemy, in a place
where we could produce no impression on them unless they
came out of their entrenchments, which they showed no disposition to do. Our guns were planted on a slight rise in front
of the enemy, who were on the fuse of a rugged hill on the
other side of the highway to Mexico, which passed nearly close
to their breastworks. Our troops occupied a plain covered with
large masses of lava, that afforded excellent cover to infantry
in skirmishing, and a deep ravine crossed the bottom of the
plain close to the road to Mexico. We fired twenty or thirty
rounds at bodies of the enemy whom we could see drawn up as if

they expected us to assault them immediately in front, but I think we must have been about a mile from them, as all our shots seemed to fall short. A division of the infantry under General [Persifor F.] Smith and Colonel [Bennett] Riley engaged with a body of the enemy; they kept up a brisk fire of musketry all afternoon, but without coming to close quarters; the enemy would not leave their entrenchments, and General Scott, it was evident, had not decided on the best mode of making the attack. The heavy guns of the enemy, among which were several long eighteens and twenty-four pounders, kept up an incessant fire during the whole afternoon. After the first half hour or so, the captain perceiving that our guns were useless at the distance we were from the enemy, ordered us to cease firing, bring our guns down off the elevation they were placed on, and lie down on the ground. By this time one of our officers, Lieutenant Johnstone, was mortally wounded by a cannon ball, and another poor fellow called Flentitz, a German, had his leg shot off. Another cannon ball smashed the axle of one of our pieces, dismounting it and rendering it useless for the time, while two of our horses were killed, and a number of our men and horses injured by grape. They were now beginning to get our range, and nothing but their excessively bad firing had saved our battery from being totally annihilated during the half hour in which we had served as a target, while it was evident that our six-pounders were useless. We lay therefore completely inactive during the remainder of the afternoon, under cover of the rising ground on which our battery had been placed. Indeed only a small portion of our troops were engaged, and I suspect the whole affair of the afternoon was only a feint for the purpose of discovering the easiest plan of assault.

At the commencement of the engagement, and as we were all busily employed in the loading and firing our guns, an infantry sergeant passing within a short distance of our battery, was observed to drop suddenly as if he had been struck by a shot. After the firing was over some of the men went to see if he was dead, or if any assistance could be rendered him. He appeared to have been dead for some time, but there was no mark of a wound on any part of his body. A small quantity of blood came from his mouth, nostrils, and even from his ears, and it was supposed that a large ball passing close to his head had caused his death.

At sunset the firing ceased and a heavy cold rain succeeded, lasting the whole of that night, and making it a most wretched night for a bivouac. To add to our misfortunes we were all suffering grievously from thirst, and there was no water within a mile whereof we were. About nine o'clock our captain received an order to retire on the division by the same way in which we had come. This was very foolish, as the night was so dark that it was impossible to see a yard in front. But orders whether foolish or not must be obeyed, though it is hard to hinder soldiers from grumbling, and there was plenty of it at this order, of which every one saw the absurdity. At last our men having been collected from various nooks and corners, and our guns limbered up, we commenced our singular march to the rear. After toiling for about six hours, and breaking and damaging the wheels and carriages, and utterly exhausting both men and horses in trying to force the wheels over impracticable masses of lava, we were compelled to desist after moving about four or five hundred yards. We then sat or lay down on the grass, our clothes clinging to us with wet, and the rain still pouring, yet so thoroughly were we tired with our fruitless toil that we slept soundly for two or three hours. We were roused at day-break and continued our march to the rear with comparative ease, as we now could distinguish objects for a few yards round us, and before sunrise we had gained the division.

The rain had now ceased, and about ten minutes after our arrival at the division several shots were heard from the enemy's battery followed by a brisk fire of musketry. On getting up on the top of our caisson boxes we could see a body of infantry approaching the flank nearest San Augustine of the enemy's position. They advanced at a quick pace loading and firing as they advanced, and receiving a fire of musketry from the Mexican infantry. But none of the guns of the battery could be brought to bear upon them; the Mexicans had been completely taken by surprise, never having dreamed of an assault in that direction. As our infantry approached within a hundred or two hundred yards of their breastworks, we could see the Mexicans break and run in the utmost confusion, scrambling over the breastworks and out on the road to Mexico. Such was the battle of Contreras; and the time occupied in the assault, in which about two hundred volunteers and half disciplined soldiers, routed thrice their number of Mexican troops stationed behind formidable entrenchments, was about five minutes.

The brigade of General Smith, principally composed of volunteers, have the credit of this assault. These troops had been marched by a long and difficult route in the wet dark night to a position where they lay ready to flank and surprise the enemy as soon as it became sufficiently light for operations. Colonel Riley and General Smith led their men gallantly to the assault, which cost the assaulting party a merely trifling loss in killed and wounded compared with the enemy, who are said to have had upwards of 700 killed on the field. About 1800 prisoners were taken, and eighteen guns, besides an immense quantity of ammunition.

The whole of our troops were immediately put in motion to follow up the success by pursuing the flying enemy towards the city of Mexico. As for our battery our captain considered it necessary to allow the horses a rest, as they were so weak from the exertions of the previous day and night, that they could scarcely stand. We remained therefore in the neighbourhood of Contreras until the afternoon, most of the men lying on the grass, and sleeping undisturbed by the ceaseless booming of the cannon and roll of musketry which told us of another engagement four or five miles in front.

About five miles from Contreras on the highway to the city, Santa Anna had strongly fortified a small village called Churubusco. This, our division, which had followed up the flying enemy from Contreras, assisted General Worth's division in carrying after an obstinate resistance, which lasted five or six hours. The loss suffered by our army at this battle of Churubusco amounted to 500 in killed and wounded, of whom a more than usual proportion were officers. The regiment to which I belonged had five officers killed and several wounded in this engagement; among the killed were Captains Burke and Capron, the former of whom enlisted me, the latter had charge of the company to which I belonged until promoted a few months before to the captaincy of another company. Among the prisoners taken at this engagement were seventy deserters from the American army. They were tried by a general Court Martial shortly after the battle, and being found guilty of the crime of desertion were sentenced to be hung, which sentence was carried into execution in presence of a portion of the troops shortly before we entered the city. I sincerely pitied these poor fellows, many of whom I had reason to believe had been driven to the foolish step they had taken by harsh and cruel usage, operating on a sensitive and excitable temperament. The barbarous treatment which soldiers sometimes received from ignorant and brutal officers, and non-commissioned officers, on that campaign, were I to relate it in minute detail, would seem almost incredible. I have frequently seen foolish young officers violently strike and assault soldiers on the most slight provocation; while to tie them up by the wrist, as high as their hands would reach, with a gag in their mouths, was a common punishment for trivial offences. In fact such a bad state of feeling seemed to exist between men and officers throughout the service that I was not surprised that it should lead to numerous desertions. If our men had not known how utterly wretched was the condition of soldiers in the Mexican service, deserting to which was literally jumping out of the frying-pan into the fire, I believe that numerous as these desertions were they would have been infinitely more so. These deserters were considered a principal cause of the obstinate resistance which our troops met at Churubusco, two or three attempts of the Mexicans to hoist a white flag having been frustrated by some of them, who killed the Mexicans attempting to display it. The large number of officers killed in the affair was also ascribed to them, as for the gratification of their revenge they aimed at no other objects during the engagement.

In the evening our battery moved to Churubusco, and next day we were sent along with our division to a small village called Miscoac, about two miles from Churubusco, and about the same distance, four miles, from the city. There we were quartered in one end of a church, a regiment of infantry called Voltigeurs, occupying the other end. A few days after the battle, Santa Anna and General Scott agreed to an armistice, the former General pretending that he was inclined to come to terms and conclude the war on the basis of an honourable treaty of peace. For agreeing to this armistice General Scott was much blamed at the time by many of the men, as it was said that we could easily have taken the city if we had followed up our success after the battles of Contreras and Churubusco. I have no doubt that we could have done so, although I am inclined to think that the difficulty of restraining our troops from the commission of excess, would have been much greater if our success had been followed up at that time. A collision between the mass of the inhabitants and our troops in that case would most likely have ensued, which would have engendered a hostile spirit of opposition that might have embittered and prolonged the war, of which the Americans were now almost as tired as the Mexicans. By showing a desire for peace after these victories, he secured the good will of many of the influential inhabitants, and I believe it is chiefly owing to the spirit of conciliation and moderation displayed by General Scott throughout the whole of the campaign that America owes the speedy and honourable termination of the war.

The principal terms of the armistice were that neither army should erect any fortifications nor receive any reinforcements of troops without giving the other army forty-eight hours' notice. Our army was also to be furnished with supplies of provisions and forage from the city. But Santa Anna, who only wanted to gain time, had thousands of soldiers employed in digging ditches and making fortifications of earth at various points of the city, parties of them working day and night under his own direction. About the fourth or fifth of August a party of our waggons, in agreement with one of the conditions of the armistice, having been sent into the city for supplies of forage and provisions, the drivers were attacked by a crowd of people with stones, and a number of them severely injured. A party of Mexican soldiers were tardily sent to their rescue, who protected them out of the city. General Scott now declared the armistice to be at an end.

On the morning of the 9th of August [September 8, 1847], General Worth's division, which was quartered at Tacubaya, according to orders, previously received, proceeded to make an attack on *Molino del Rey* (The King's mill). The enemy, it was believed, had a foundry for casting cannons there, besides a great quantity of military stores. It was also considered necessary to have it in possession before proceeding to the reduction of Chapultepec, to which it formed a strong outwork. The attack commenced a little before sunrise, but the enemy having been informed of this early visit, had drawn all their troops from the city during the night, who were posted in the most advantageous manner. Accordingly on the advance of our troops they received a most destructive fire, which compelled them to fall back, leaving the field covered with their killed and wounded. The Mexican lancers exhibited most characteristically both their cowardice and cruelty of disposition on this occasion, by riding out and killing the wounded who were lying on the field, while they never attempted to follow up the broken line of infantry who had been compelled to retire. But our troops though discouraged were not beaten, and after a fight of two hours, the Mexicans, who were at least four times their number, retreated, leaving them in possession of the field. The victory, though proving the immense superiority of our troops to those of the enemy, was a dear one, our loss in killed and wounded being between eight and nine hundred out of a force engaged numbering little more than three thousand.

About an hour after the commencement of the action our

battery was ordered to be got ready and to hurry out to the ground. Miscoac, where we lay, is about four miles from *Molino del Rey*, and the road being rough and up hill a good part of the way, it took us nearly an hour to reach it. One of our men not holding on firmly while galloping over the rough road was thrown off the caisson box, and a wheel passing over his body broke two or three of his ribs and otherwise severely injured him. But our battery was short of men, and the captain could spare nobody to attend him, so he was left by the roadside in a seemingly dying state. He recovered, however, and was discharged in consequence of the internal injuries he had received. As we entered the battle ground we met a number of waggons returning with wounded, and a few wounded soldiers walking slowly, assisted by one or two comrades. There was an occasional gun fired from the castle of Chapultepec, and a party of our infantry kept up a skirmishing fire with a few of the enemy who were in the woods round the hill on which the castle is built, but the battle was evidently over. We unlimbered our guns and fired several shots at a large body of lancers who were hovering on our left flank, when they suddenly wheeled to the right-about. "I wish, captain, you would let them come a little nearer the next time; you scared them rather too soon," said General Cadwallader, who came up as the lancers rode off. A powder magazine belonging to the enemy, but in our possession at the time, blew up with a tremendous explosion, killing and wounding a great number of our men who were in its vicinity. We remained on the field, with several regiments of infantry and cavalry, until about noon, when we received orders to retire.

On the morning of the 12th of August [September] our battery moved along with General Pillow's division to the field of *Molino del Rey;* our division being stationed there for the purpose of protecting a heavy battery advantageously planted in the vicinity for the bombardment of Chapultepec. This castle, a strong stone building, well furnished with artillery and ammunition, is built on the top of an insulated rocky hill,

wooded from the base about half way up. As it commanded
the entrance to the city on that side, it was considered essential
that it should be taken. At daybreak on the morning of the
12th, our mortars opened on it and continued to throw heavy
shells into it until night, by which time the havoc among the
troops inside must have been very great, judging from the appearance of the building after the action. After the firing had
ceased in the evening General Pillow addressed his men, telling
them that they were to assault the castle early next morning,
when he said he had no doubt they would easily carry it at the
point of the bayonet in less than half an hour; which intimation
the soldiers received with three cheers.

The duty assigned our battery was to approach the bottom
of the hill of Chapultepec and throw in shells and round shot
into the wood and up the face of the hill, for the purpose of
driving in the enemy and affording a footing to our assaulting
party. We accordingly placed our guns that evening in the
position they were to occupy next morning, and shortly after
sunrise we received orders to commence firing. An ill-directed
fire of musketry from the enemy's outlying piquets stationed
in the woods, reached us as we commenced firing, slightly
wounding several of our men. But a few shells thrown in the
right direction soon removed that source of annoyance, and
where we were the guns of the castle could not be depressed
sufficiently to bear on us. We continued to fire until we had
thrown over a hundred shots into the grounds, when we were
told to cease firing and allow the infantry to advance. Two or
three regiments of infantry, among whom I recognised the
regiment of Voltigeurs who had been stationed with us in the
church since the battle of Contreras, now advanced, some of
them carrying a ladder between two of them besides their guns
and bayonets. To get into the grounds they had to scale a wall
about six or seven feet high, and with the aid of the ladders
they were soon all over, and advancing under cover of the
huge trees towards the open rocky ground half way up the
hill.

While the action was going on here at Chapultepec, a strangely horrible scene was being enacted under General Twiggs at Miscoac, the small town in which our division had been quartered during the armistice. Twenty of the deserters who were taken at Churubusco had been brought out on a plain for execution, General Twiggs commanding the troops appointed to witness the sentence carried into effect. From the plain where they were to be executed they had a view of the castle of Chapultepec about three miles distant, and could hear the sound of the firing, and see distinctly the smoke of the guns and muskets of its defenders and assailants, and here they were launched into eternity.

While the infantry advanced on the castle we hitched the horses into the battery and stood waiting to pursue the enemy, who we were confident would not make a long resistance, as the bombardment of the previous day had done great execution on the building. The firing from the castle soon commenced on our assaulting party, who at first suffered severely, but after about two hours' hard fighting they scaled the steep ascent and drove the enemy from the ramparts. General [Nicolás] Bravo and several hundred of the Mexican soldiers were taken prisoners in the castle. The remainder of the garrison escaped by the opposite side of the castle from which our troops entered, and ran in confusion along the highway to the city. Just as we commenced to follow in pursuit, a shower of grape from the castle killed two horses and wounded several others, while almost miraculously their riders did not receive the slightest injury. The shot came from a gun at an angle of the castle, which continued to fire for some time after our men had gained the ramparts, and until our men had shot down the most of those who were working it. This delayed our battery several minutes until we cut the harness and hauled the horses to one side of the road. Near the place where this accident occurred the enemy had cut a trench across the road, which delayed us some time until it was filled up. While a party of infantry were at work filling up the trench, two citizens of the class called army followers rode over to where three Mexican

soldiers were endeavouring to conceal themselves behind some
bushes about a quarter of a mile off the road. The Mexicans,
who were probably wounded and unable to fly with the rest
of the garrison, got upon their knees in the attitude of suppli-
cation, when these inhuman scoundrels deliberately shot them
down by firing repeated shots of their revolvers. A loud
murmur of disapprobation at this atrociously savage act burst
from the soldiers on the road who observed it, and a ball from
an infantry soldier's musket whistled past their ears as they
approached the road. On their return they received a shower
of curses and epithets, showing the detestation in which their
infamous conduct was held.

The ditch being filled up we continued the pursuit of the
flying enemy, and as we went at a fast gallop we had soon
left the infantry far behind, and found ourselves entirely un-
supported. A large body of the enemy's cavalry were now
perceived advancing on us from the city; we immediately unlimbered and began to fire shell and round shot among them
with the utmost rapidity, when they made a precipitate retreat.
Several riderless horses scouring wildly over the fields on our
left, which none of them stayed to catch, and which were
valuable prizes to some of our infantry afterwards, showed us
that our firing had made an impression, and explained the reason of their sudden change of purpose. If these lancers had
charged us boldly, they could have cut us to pieces and taken
possession of our battery with ease, as we had no support
within a mile of us. Our company only numbered at that time
about sixty men, armed with sabres, which none of them knew
how to use, and which would have been a poor defence
against their lances. A body of cavalry and infantry arriving
soon after, we continued our march until we arrived at the
suburbs of the city. Here our battery and a regiment of infantry were posted to defend a road leading to Toluca, on
which a large body of the enemy's cavalry had been observed
moving off in the morning. Colonel Duncan's battery and a
regiment of infantry were now engaged in driving the enemy
from the San Cosme gate, half a mile nearer the city. Here the

enemy had a breastwork of earth built across the road, behind which were two nine-pounders. There was also a mortar on the flat roof of a house on the left of the gate, several shells from which dropped into our position, killing and wounding a number of the infantry stationed with us to defend the entrance to the city from Toluca. This was also carried after two or three hours' fighting, leaving us in complete possession of that entrance to the city.

Generals Worth and Quitman had commenced their attack on the opposite side of the city early in the morning, and after driving the enemy from several of their outworks in succession, had succeeded after a severe fight in carrying the citadel by assault. The latter was the enemy's stronghold, where they had a strong battery of heavy guns, and after it was taken the Mexican troops retired in disorder from the city by the Peñon and Guadaloupe gates, having utterly abandoned all idea of further resistance. Their large army of 18,000 men was now completely scattered and disorganized, and this by a force not exceeding one-third of their number, acting as assailants, and having to drive them from strong fortifications. Santa Anna, according to his usual custom, retired with a strong body of cavalry before our troops had gained possession of the citadel. He has not entered the capital since, and I question if all his cunning will ever be sufficient to reinstate him in the good opinions of any large or influential class of his countrymen again. Some desultory fighting took place on the following day, the 14th, between our troops and parties of patriots, principally criminals who had been released from their cells and stationed in the steeples of churches for the purpose. These were soon quelled, and before night the city was perfectly quiet, and considered quite securely in our possession. General Scott entered the city on the 14th, the day after the battle of Chapultepec and the storming of the citadel. By his excellent arrangements in quartering his troops in the suburbs for a few days, he succeeded in securing order, and preserving his men from those excesses which might have been apprehended from the description of troops under his command.

CHAPTER 15   It Was Fierce
                              and Bloody

The man who would defeat Scott for the Presidency of the
United States in 1852 commanded a brigade on the march to
Mexico City. General Franklin Pierce of New Hampshire was
no professional soldier. A lawyer and a congressman before
the Mexican War, he had enlisted as a private in one of the
first volunteer companies raised in his state. He recounted the
action at Contreras and Churubusco in a letter to his brother.

GENERAL   FRANKLIN   PIERCE
Letter to his Brother, August 24, 1847
Franklin Pierce Papers, Library of Congress, Washington, D.C.

Aug. 24, 1847

MY DEAR BROTHER,

Since I left Vera Cruz, to this time, I have had no means of
communicating with the States. Altho but a few months in
the service, *I know* what is fatigue, anxiety & exposure. Contrary to my expectations & contrary to my orders from the
Department at Washington, I was compelled for the want of
the requisite provisions for transportation to remain more than
three weeks at Vera Cruz & more than four in *tierra caliente*
(the vomito region so called).

I left the dreaded city on the 10th of July, with 2500 men of all arms, and a train of waggons which when closed up extended more than two miles. On the 6th of August I reached Puebla without the loss of a single waggon, and with my command in fine condition. My command was attacked 6 times in the march, but the enemy's force in each instance was easily disposed with trifling loss on our side. The natural bridge afforded the enemy great natural advantages, to which they had added breastworks on a high bluff which commanded the bridge . . . ; across the main bridge they had also thrown a barricade. I soon discovered that there was no way in which his position could be turned & that my artillery was ineffective from the most commanding point where it could be placed. I determined, of course, to cross under the plunging fire of the enemy's escopets. My order to advance was admirably executed. At the moment Lt. Col. [M. L.] Bonham's Battalion rushed forward with a shout, the enemy poured down a heavy fire by which several of my men were severely wounded. Col. Bonham's horse was shot near me & a ball passed through the rim of my hat in very dangerous proximity to my face. One man leaped the barricade followed by . . . [a] company of cavalry, and in less than 10 minutes the enemy was in flight in every direction, and the American flag moved upon the high bluff which they had occupied. The Mexican force consisted, as they said afterwards, of 500 men. Had they possessed courage & skill in the use of arms, our loss must have been very great.

You can hardly conceive the strength of the natural defenses of the road over which we passed. Rumors came to me almost every night that we would be attacked by large forces the next day, but they made nowhere, any thing like a brave & stern resistance. The official reports of the great battle of Mexico will probably reach you as soon as this letter, and I shall therefore not attempt to give the minute details. It was fierce & bloody beyond any thing that has occurred in this war. The battle differed in many respects from that of Buena

Vista. There General Taylor received the enemy in a strong position selected by himself.

Our force on the 20th consisted of less than 9000 men. The Mexican force within supporting distance & engaged, undoubtedly exceeded 30,000. We attacked him in position on ground of his own selection, admirably fortified.

You will distinguish so far as numbers are concerned between the battle of the morning & that of the afternoon — altho spoken of in official report as one engagement under the designation of the "Battle of Mexico." We took during the day thirty five pieces of artillery — an immense amount of ammunition, 800 mules & horses — more than 2000 prisoners, among them 8 Generals and any number of Colonels. The Mexican loss in killed & wounded must have been immense. Our troops killed 500 Mexicans upon the field of battle, commenced in the morning at Contreras, and the loss in the afternoon was much greater. Our loss too has been heavy. With this small army we could not afford to purchase many such victories at such a price. One of the Regiments of my brigade (the 15th) lost in killed & wounded one third of its entire force. In killed & wounded we number not less than 1000, and among them I lament to say an unusual proportion of valuable officers. The Maryland Regiment suffered severely & behaved throughout in the most gallant manner. My horse at full speed, on the evening of the 19th when leading my Brigade thru a perfect storm of round shot & shells, fell under me upon a ledge of rock, by which I sustained a severe injury by the shock & fright but especially by a severe sprain in my left knee which came under him. At first I was not conscious of any serious injury but soon became exceedingly faint when Dr. Ritcher, surgeon of the 12th (a portion of my command) who was following the advancing column closely overtook me & administered to me as well as he could under the circumstances. In a few minutes I was able to walk with difficulty & pressed forward to Capt. [John Bankhead] Magruder's Battery, where I found the horse of poor gallant Lt. Johnson who had just received a mortal wound of which he died that evening. I was permitted to take him (my arm having been totally disabled), was helped into the saddle & continued in it until 11 o'clock that night. It was exceedingly dark, the rain poured in torrents, & being separated from my servants & baggage I was without hat or covering. Add to this that during the afternoon of the 19th, we had gained an advantage over the enemy who remained firmly entrenched with 7000 men opposed to 4000, on our side without the possibility of bringing our Artillery to bear, & you will readily conceive that our situation was not the most agreeable. The morning of the 20th however was as brilliant as the night of the 19th had been dark & gloomy.

Soon after day light the enemy's works were carried with the bayonet and of their 7000 men, regular troops under the command of Genl. Valencia, probably 4000 cannot be found today. As we passed this field in pursuit of the fugitives the scene was awful. The road & adjacent fields every where strewn with the mangled bodies of the dead & dying. We continued the pursuit until one o'clock when our front came up with the enemy's strong works at Churubusco and San Antonio, when the great conflict of the P.M. commenced.

At San Angel dispositions having been made to attack in reverse the enemy's works on the San Augustin road Genl. Scott ordered me to march my Brigade in concert with that of the intrepid Genl. Shields across the open country between Santa Catarina and the above named road in order to cut off the enemy's retreat.

We gained the position sought and although the enemy's line was perfectly formed & extended as far as the eye could reach in either direction they were attacked vigorously & successfully. Arriving at a ditch which it was impossible for my horse to leap, I dismounted & hurried forward, without thinking of my injury, at the head of my Brigade for 200 or 300 yards, when turning suddenly upon my knee the cartilage of which had been seriously injured, I fainted & fell upon the bank in the direct range & within perfect reach of the enemy's fire. That I escaped seems to me now providential. The rout & overthrow of the whole Mexican force soon became complete & we could easily have taken the city, but Genl. Scott was met with a proposition for an armistice (after demanding the surrender of the city) with a view to open negotiations for peace. In my judgment the Army, full of ardor & confidence, was humanely & wisely restrained. Major Genl. Quitman, Genl. Persifor F. Smith & myself were appointed Commissioners to meet the Mexican Commissioners to settle the terms of the armistice. Although I had not taken off my spurs or slept an hour for two nights in consequence of my engagements & the pain in my knee, I obeyed the summons, was helped into my saddle & rode 2½ miles to Tacubaya where the Commission assembled at the house of Mr. McIntosh, the British consul general. Our conference commenced late in the afternoon and at 4 o'clock the next morning the Articles were signed. That I was pretty thoroughly exhausted you will readily imagine. I slept an hour or two that morning at Genl. Worth's quarters and my sprained knee which was by far my most serious injury has been daily improving and today I ride without much inconvenience. I have lost several dear friends although our acquaintance had been of short duration. I visited the Hospital yesterday & saw officers & men with shot in all parts of their persons, although all who were not really dying seemed cheerful and many who had lost limbs in high spirits, still I sickened at the sight.

My general health has been good. I have been either in my saddle or on my feet every day since I left Vera Cruz, which can be said by few in my command, for almost all were obliged at some portion of the march, in consequence of the change of climate, water, exposure &c, to avail themselves of the ambulance. Col. [S. E.] Watson with his Marine Corps accompanied me & has been uniformly well. He is an excellent, agreeable gentleman & admirable officer, and I regret that having been left with Gen. Quitman's division at San Augustin, he had no opportunity to participate in the Battle of the 19th & 20th. Now a word with regard to the great object of this War — "Peace." There is no doubt that Santa Anna is sincerely desirous of Peace. Commissioners to treat have been appointed and met Mr. [Nicholas B.] Trist this afternoon at 4 o'clock. My belief is, that Peace will be the result although no man can speak with confidence. My thoughts are almost constantly of Home, and the dear ones there. How I long to see them, even if I hear from them, is impossible for me to express. In case of peace I shall avail myself of the earliest moment consistent with my Duty and Honor to return to the States & to resume the great pursuit of private life.

CHAPTER 16

A Glorious
Triumph

During the American drive inland General Scott relied heavily upon his engineers for reconnaissance and topographical advice. One of the most energetic of these young engineers was Lieutenant Isaac Ingalls Stevens (1818–1862), who was graduated at the head of his West Point class in 1839 and later served as governor of Washington Territory and as a Union general. Stevens revealed some of his experiences in an extended letter to his wife.

LIEUTENANT ISAAC INGALLS STEVENS
Letter to his wife, in
Hazard Stevens, The Life of Isaac Ingalls Stevens, *2 vols.*
Boston, Houghton Mifflin & Co., 1900, Vol. I, pp. 188–201

August 22, 1847

MY DEAREST WIFE

The great battle of Mexico has been fought, and our arms have achieved a glorious triumph. Commissions are now sitting to treat of an armistice that will terminate, as we all trust, in a permanent and honorable peace to both countries. Mexico is again without an army, and the gates of the capital are open to us. Terrible was the conflict, severe our loss, particularly in efficient and gallant officers; the whole army was engaged, and the whole public force of Mexico struck down, large numbers of prisoners and a great amount of material of war falling into our hands.

My heart is filled with gratitude to the Most High that I had the strength to do my duty with the other officers of my corps, and that, although much exposed in three different reconnoisances and two hard-fought battles, I have escaped without a wound, and without any abatement of my health and strength. I cannot feel exultation. We have lost many brave officers and men, some my personal friends; streams of blood have in reality flowed over the battlefield. The hearts of the whole Mexican nation are thrilling with anguish and dismay. Such is war, so glittering and imposing on parade and in anticipation, so terrible in reality.

Puebla is about seventy-five miles from Mexico. On referring to the map, you will find that the direct road passes between lakes Tezcuco on the north, Chalco and Xochimilco on the south. At the Venta de Chalco, about twenty miles from Mexico, the road turns off to pass southward of the lakes. El Peñon, about eight miles from Mexico, is a high hill entirely surrounded with water, along the edge of which the great direct road to Mexico passes, consisting of a causeway for about a mile and approaching it, and also of a causeway the whole distance after leaving it, till we reach the City of Mexico.

General Twiggs with his splendid division was in the advance, followed on successive days by Quitman, Worth, and Pillow. In five days Twiggs was pushed up to Ayotla, fifteen or sixteen miles from Mexico, General Scott continuing with him in the advance, and the other divisions five, fifteen, and twenty-five miles in rear. As they came up (it required two days), they were held in reserve at the head of Lake Chalco, whilst the proper reconnoissances and examinations were made to determine the general plan of attack. The first day, a reconnoissance was made of the Peñon, supported by a squadron of dragoons, a regiment of infantry, and two pieces of artillery. The Peñon was found to be fortified and occupied in force. Captain [James L.] Mason, of the engineers (my friend Mason), Major Gaines, of the Kentucky volunteers (taken prisoner just before the great battle of Buena Vista, and who made his escape only one or two days before the march of the army from Puebla), and myself rode some distance in the advance, and observed near the causeway some eight or ten Mexican officers. We were at least three quarters of a mile from the rest of our force. We advanced upon them, they curveting their horses and advancing upon us. When within about three hundred yards they discharged their pistols, but we continuing our advance, they all turned their horses and returned full speed across the causeway, carrying with them a troop of lancers. The whole affair was very amusing and afforded much sport. It did not diminish our contempt of Mexican prowess.

The second day a splendid reconnoissance was made of the whole country between the lakes, including the Peñon and Mexicalcingo at the head of Lake Xochimilco. The particular reconnoissance of the Peñon was intrusted to me. On my little horse, one of the most enduring, spirited, and beautiful animals in the service, with two dragoons, I went half way around the Peñon, and was for seven hours within almost point-blank range of its guns, examining the different batteries, determining the various approaches, and particularly the character of the inundation. Frequently I was in the water up to the belly of my horse. General Scott was very much pleased with my reconnoissance, and I got more credit for it than I deserved. The same day Mason made an admirable reconnoissance of Mexicalcingo.

Our spies had given information that the road around Chalco was impracticable for our trains, and in consequence thereof the General almost made up his mind to force Mexicalcingo, and at that point and westward, fight the great battle of the war. He, however, determined to wait one day for additional information.

Worth, who had now come up, was sent to Chalco, and a column under the orders of Colonel Duncan reconnoitred the road around the lakes. Our spies were found to have given wrong information, and the road, though bad, was found to be practicable. That same evening General Scott, with the whole field before him, determined to move around Chalco, and ordered the movement to commence on the morrow.

The prompt advance of Twiggs to Ayotla, the brigade of dragoons of the famous Colonel Harney two miles farther in advance, and the brilliant reconnoissances of the two succeeding days impressed the enemy with the belief that the Peñon was to be attacked, and they lost no time in filling the place with troops, and putting in position formidable batteries of nearly forty guns.

In the movement around the lakes Worth was in the advance, followed by Pillow, Quitman, and Twiggs. The road was exceedingly bad and narrow, in many places a perfect defile, obstructed by cuts, stones from the hills in some cases formed into walls, and requiring great patience, energy, and perseverance for the passage of the trains.

The third day Worth reached San Augustin, General Scott and staff resting at Xochimilco with the divisions of Pillow, Quitman, and Twiggs respectively some five and ten miles in rear; no obstruction of moment occurring either in front or rear, unless we except a demonstration of a large force of lancers on the movement of General Twiggs's division from Ayotla, a demonstration brought speedily to a close by the opening of Taylor's battery.

Early the next morning, Wednesday, August 18, Scott joined Worth; developed his general plan of attack, and ordered the engineers immediately to make vigorous reconnoissances of the position and force of the enemy. He remarked, "To-day the enemy may feel us, to-morrow we must feel him."

Accordingly two reconnoissances were made, — one, of the position of San Antonio, three miles from San Augustin, on the great southern road to Mexico, conducted by Major [John L.] Smith; the other, of the road to San Angel, turning the position of San Antonio, and bringing us to the next great and adjacent causeway to the west. This latter reconnoissance was conducted by Captain [Robert E.] Lee.

The first reconnoissance was supported by the whole of Worth's division. Captain Mason had charge of one party, I had charge of the other. Whilst the whole party of engineer officers with a portion of the escort were examining the position of San Antonio within twelve hundred yards of its guns, and in the causeway itself, the enemy discharged his battery of two large brass 16-pounders, blowing to pieces the body of the gallant Captain Thornton, commanding the escort, and severely wounding an interpreter. The second reconnoitring party (that of Captain Lee) were brought into pretty close contact with a body of the enemy, whom they completely dispersed without any loss. Thus, the enemy felt us the first day. Pillow and Quitman had now come up to San Augustin (ten miles from Mexico), and Twiggs to Xochimilco, four miles in rear.

It was determined to move the main body on San Angel, Worth remaining in front of San Antonio, and by a vigorous combined movement forcing this position and advancing upon Tacubaya.

Accordingly, on Thursday Pillow and Twiggs were pushed forward over a most difficult road, requiring much labor to make it practicable for field-guns, and in full view of a large force of the enemy, who, divining our intentions from the reconnoissance of Wednesday, had intrenched himself in a strong position, barring our passage. As our troops approached, they were brought gallantly into action. [Lt. Franklin D.] Callender's howitzer battery was advanced to a very exposed position for the temporary purpose of driving in a picket, was not withdrawn in time, and, exposed to a formidable battery of twelve guns, was entirely cut up, its gallant commander receiving severe wounds in both legs. Magruder's battery of 12-pounders was in like manner advanced and cut up. These batteries were supported by Smith's brigade on the left, and the 9th infantry on the right. The 9th infantry I led across an open field, exposed to the enemy's grape, without the loss of a man. They advanced to a strong position in a ravine, which they maintained till dark.

Riley's brigade and the greater portion of Pillow's division were pushed forward against the enemy's right to cut him off from his reserve, and by a vigorous charge take him in flank and hurl him into the gorges of the mountains.

The whole field of approach was a perfect honeycomb of lava projections, entirely impracticable for horse and difficult for foot. Nothing was known of the ground. All the troops advanced with difficulty. That intrepid veteran, Riley, with his gallant brigade, pushed forward and encountered the enemy's lancers in large force, repulsing them in successive charges. He organized his brigade to charge the battery, but felt it his duty to await orders and support.

Smith, somewhat late in the day withdrawn from the right, reached a village on the left of the enemy's position, to which Riley had withdrawn, and was reinforced by the greater portion of Shields's and a portion of Pierce's brigade. An attack under the direction of Smith was organized, but could not be executed in consequence of the gathering shadows of the night.

At this moment, all offensive operations on our side having ceased and no impression made on the enemy's line, their reserves coming up in great force and bringing with them additional guns, cheer on cheer rose from their whole line, whilst on our part there was much gloom and despondency. Our commands were much scattered, our batteries had become disabled, and every one was overcome with the fatigues of the day. During the latter part of the day I was reconnoitring in the advanced position of the 9th infantry, and, not knowing the progress of the day in other parts of the field, returned to the rear for orders. I found General Pillow, who seemed somewhat perplexed with the posture of affairs, and gave me no orders till dark was coming on. I endeavored to find my way back, but could not succeed. I was so entirely exhausted that it was with the greatest difficulty that I could drag one foot after the other. Finally I fell upon a small party of rifles and 9th infantry, led by Lieutenant [John Gray] Foster, of the engineers, who were making good their retreat from a house somewhat higher up on the same stream with the position of the 9th infantry, and from which they had been expelled by a whole regiment of the enemy. On hailing the party, Foster recognized my voice, and I concluded to return with him, but so entirely worn down that I required his support. We made our way with great difficulty, occasionally meeting little parties of soldiers seeking their commands. It had already commenced raining. On passing near the place where I left my horse, I could not find him, and was obliged to pursue my way on foot. At length we reached some dragoons near the foot of a hill, where General Scott had placed himself to observe the field, and there learned that he had left half an hour before for San Augustin, three miles distant. I inquired for my horse, but could not find him. Foster kindly lent me his, and after waiting some half an hour I set out on my return to San Augustin in company with Captain Sibley's troop of dragoons.

On my way back my feelings were not desponding, but I was sad. The 9th infantry, called the New England regiment, who had gallantly followed my lead, and had occupied for hours an exposed position, I had not succeeded in bringing back to the place indicated by the general. I felt deeply my physical inability to support long-continued exertion. It seemed to me that I had abandoned a body of men who were relying on me. The regiment had acted nobly, and none more so than Pitman, acting as major. He was cool and intrepid throughout.

On my way home the rain poured in torrents much of the time. I overtook my intrepid friend Callender, whom some men of his company were carrying home on a litter. He seemed to be comfortable, and is now rapidly recovering from his wound.

On reaching my quarters, getting some supper, and changing my clothes, I went to see General Scott. He was surrounded by his personal staff, and was attentively listening to Captain Lee's account of the state of the field. Soon after, General Pillow and General Twiggs entered the room. Twiggs is a gray-haired veteran of sixty, large in person, of rather blunt address, and of little advantages in education, but possessing in an eminent degree decision of character, great sagacity as to men and events, and an aptitude for labor. He has the most splendid division in the service, the fruit in great measure of his own unwearied exertions. Captain Lee is an officer of engineers to whom I have before alluded, and one of my messmates. He is one of the most extraordinary men in the service. In the very prime of manhood, of remarkable presence and address, perhaps the most manly and striking officer in the service, of great grace of manner and great personal beauty, he has established an enduring reputation. His power of enduring fatigue is extraordinary, and his strength of judgment and perfect balance are conspicuous. For counsel, General Scott relies more upon him than any other man in the service.

I never shall forget that evening, — Captain Lee in calm, even, well-weighed words, giving a full view of the state of our force, suggesting the various methods of reëstablishing affairs, and proffering his own services and exertions to carry out the views of the general; Scott, composed, complacent, weighing every word he said, finding fault with no one's blunders, and taking in all cases the best view of things, indulging in no apprehensions, and exhibiting entire confidence in the ultimate event. At length General Twiggs and Captain Lee returned to the battlefield with full powers to retrieve affairs as their best judgment should dictate. It had been proposed by General Smith, one of Twiggs's brigadiers, to make a night attack upon the enemy's position, defended by twelve guns and five thousand of their best troops. Captain Lee's principal object in seeing the general was to procure his sanction. It was not denied. On returning to the field, all arrangements were made to carry it into execution.

My dear wife, I am spinning out a long letter, and I must be more brief. This night attack, in consequence of rain and the difficult nature of the ground, was not carried into execution till dawn of day. It was organized by General Smith. The reconnoissance of the route was made in the night by my friend [Lt. Zealous B.] Tower, of the engineers. The principal column of attack consisted of Riley's brigade led by Tower. Two other columns were pushed in the same general direction, one of which was commanded by our friend Major [Justin] Dimick. The front of a column was formed of the scattered commands, mostly new levies.

Riley's column pursued its way over slippery and uneven ground, crossing two deep ravines, halting from time to time to keep the command together. Finally it reached the brow of a hill in rear of the enemy's position, and was formed in two columns, just as the coming day disclosed them to the enemy. Immediately the charge was ordered, and the gallant brigade made its terrible charge, ably supported by the other columns. The contest was brief but decisive. In fifteen minutes one thousand dead and wounded of the enemy lay on the field, nearly a thousand more were taken prisoners, and the remainder were flying in all directions. Every one speaks in the most exalted terms of the conduct of Tower. Some say he led the brigade and did the whole work.

As for myself, broken down the evening before, greatly in need of rest, I complied with the advice of Major Smith and Captain Lee and remained in town, giving directions to my servant to be called at three, in order that I might return to the field to be in season for the fight. My servant did not wake me till five. One delay after another occurred, and I was finally detained by General Scott to conduct to the field a brigade of General Worth's command. We started and had got half way out, when information came of the brilliant success of the night attack, and the brigade was ordered back. I continued my way, and finally came across Tower very quietly eating his breakfast in company with Lieutenant [P. G. T.] Beauregard of our corps, who was also conspicuous in the same attack. I rode on, passed over the battlefield, reached the advance, and exchanged greetings with my friends of the 9th regiment, who had felt as anxious for me as I had for them. They informed me that they had withdrawn to a safe place about nine in the evening, and were engaged in the night attack. My friends of the 1st artillery, Major Dimick, Captains Capron, Burke, etc., I also shook warmly by the hand, and finally rode up to General Twiggs. I congratulated him on the brilliant victory achieved by his command. "General Smith deserves the whole credit, but it was my division," was his reply.

The order was soon given to advance upon the San Antonio road, General Twiggs in advance, the object being to cause the enemy to evacuate it and open the way for the advance of Worth. I accompanied the advance. We soon reached the village of Coyoacan, from which a picket of about two hundred lancers was expelled. There we halted till General Scott rode up. He proposed to wait half an hour to reconnoitre, determine the position of the enemy, and the proper mode of attack. General Worth had previously received orders not to attack the enemy till he heard the fire on the other line.

Calling for the engineer officers, Captain Lee was directed, after examining a prisoner, to communicate with General Worth at San Antonio, and I went to the steeple of the church to use my glass. I turned it upon the San Antonio road, and observed the enemy in full retreat, the causeway for more than a mile being filled with troops, pack-mules, and baggage-wagons. I immediately reported the fact to General Scott, who ordered Twiggs to advance, and directed me to accompany his division. Twiggs pushed on, and I went forward with the officers of the engineer company to reconnoitre. We came to a fork of a road. I took to the right, Lieutenant [George B.] McClellan to the left. Mine passed directly in front of a strong building (a church), occupied in force by the enemy; his led directly to the building. At a little distance before me I saw the enemy in retreat, and we took one prisoner, who informed us that the place was defended by two guns.

My dear wife, perhaps I had not better at this time go into the details of the most terrible fight of the war, which now commenced. General Twiggs has said publicly that by my reconnoissance and efforts it was brought on, as regards his division. We all felt the strongest determination to fight the enemy, and put him to a perfect rout. At all events, it so happened that I was extremely active in pushing forward columns of attack, etc. Our friend Major Dimick's regiment I directed to its position. So with Taylor's battery. General Twiggs, in almost every case, agreed to my suggestions. By my efforts and those of the junior engineer officers, the troops were brought under fire and the battle commenced.

The veteran division of Twiggs, already engaged in two hard-fought battles, the desultory and galling conflict of the day before and the brilliant victory of the morning, exposed to the rains of the night, and the whole without the least rest from the wearisome march around Lake Chalco, came gallantly into action against the enemy, intrenched in a position of remarkable strength, — a bastioned field-work of high relief, wet ditches, armed with eight guns, some of large calibre, and protected by a church converted into a defensive building of great strength. Taylor, whom you knew in Newport, came into action in most gallant style, and opened his fire upon the enemy, driving him from the roof of the building. But so destructive was the return fire of the enemy behind his earthen breastworks that in a short time his battery was cut up, and he was obliged to withdraw, losing many men and horses, and two of his officers were wounded. Lieutenant Martin, formerly stationed in Newport, lost his arm. Riley opened his fire with great spirit and effect against the left; Smith's brigade, headed by our gallant engineer company, against the right. Worth, hearing our fire, hastened up his command, and attacked a strong bastioned field-work on the great San Antonio cause-way, and a little in rear of the work attacked by Twiggs. The 6th infantry and Duncan's battery were conducted directly up the causeway. A terrible fire of grape temporarily checked the advance of the 6th, and compelled Duncan to put his battery under cover. An attack was directed, headed by the 2d artillery, to turn the left of the position. The whole command of Worth was rushed to the attack, not in the most orderly manner, and the greatest gallantry was displayed by both officers and men. A continued blaze of fire proceeded from the extended line of the enemy, resting on the two field-works, and was returned with great spirit by both Twiggs and Worth. The roar of battle did not for a moment cease, and at times the stoutest hearts would quail.

In the mean time the brigades of Shields and Pierce, conducted by the intrepid Captain Lee, were directed around the enemy's right to get into his rear and cut off his retreat. The enemy appeared in such great force that it was with the greatest difficulty that the command could be brought to the attack. The gallant Colonel [Pierce M.] Butler, leading most nobly the Palmetto regiment, was shot dead, and Lieutenant-Colonel [John P.] Dickinson was wounded. After exceeding effort they were made to charge the enemy, the causeway was gained, and his retreat cut off. In this action both Shields and Pierce were conspicuous for their gallantry, and the latter was wounded.

Previous to the attack of Worth, the work attacked by Twiggs had been nearly silenced by the destructive fire of his two gallant brigades, the gunners were shot down, and the guns were served only at intervals. Still the church held out, and the line in rear was not touched. Worth, after one repulse and at heavy loss, took by assault the work on the causeway, the guns of which, together with two from Duncan's battery, were opened upon the work attacked by Twiggs. Shields and Pierce had now cut the causeway. Seeing no hope of escape, the white flag was hung out, and immediately the division of

Twiggs occupied the work, taking over one thousand prisoners, of whom three were general officers.

The panic was now universal. Our troops pushed forward on the great causeway, the dragoons in hot pursuit, sabring the enemy in their path. They fled in all directions. The gallant Captain [Philip] Kearny charged up almost to the very walls of the city, receiving a severe wound in the arm, which rendered its amputation necessary.

This is a meagre account of this terrible fight, more protracted and severe than anything seen at the Resaca, at Monterey, or the Cerro Gordo. Our loss is great, some forty officers in killed and wounded, and over seven hundred rank and file; nearly half the officers of the 1st artillery were killed or wounded. Major Dimick commanded the regiment in three battles and escaped without a wound.

As I have before said, I was on duty with the division of Twiggs. This veteran was greatly exposed during the whole contest, and was conspicuous for his coolness and judgment. General Scott himself was wounded. The chief engineer, Major Smith, was also conspicuous for gallantry and good conduct. Our gallant engineer company nobly sustained its reputation as the first company in the service. At the close of the action General Scott rode over the whole field, speaking words of encouragement to the wounded, and addressing the several regiments as he passed them. On all sides he was received with the greatest enthusiasm. His words were the eloquence of the heart, and told with great effect.

General Scott and staff returned to San Augustin, some five miles from the battlefield, to pass the night. We were all greatly in need of rest. To our great satisfaction, on comparing notes it was found that not a single engineer officer had been touched, and only three soldiers of the company wounded.

Notwithstanding the great fatigues of the day, I slept little that night. The battlefield was before me with its scenes of terror and of blood. The gallant officers who fell haunted me. The loss of human life was appalling. I reflected that with less precipitation the works could have been carried with much less loss. I was precipitate like the rest, and felt in a measure culpable.

The next morning, after issuing the proper orders for the movements of the troops — orders given verbally from his horse to his aides, and with admirable precision — General Scott proceeded to the village of Coyoacan, and there met a white flag from the city. We then learned that consternation sat on that devoted place, and that her army of twenty-six thousand to thirty-two thousand men had become reduced to four thousand indifferent troops. The result of the white flag was the appointment of commissioners to treat of an armistice. This morning (Monday) the articles were duly signed, and there is now every prospect that the war has come to a close. The armistice is made by authority of the supreme government, and its avowed object is to negotiate a treaty of peace. This armistice provides generally that the two parties shall remain as they are. Hostilities are to cease within a circuit of twenty-eight leagues of the city, the guerrillas are to be withdrawn from the national road, and our communications are to be free with Vera Cruz.

MONDAY EVENING. I have sad news to-day. The first day of the armistice the Mexicans have commenced trifling with us. The armistice provided that our army should draw supplies from the city, and in consequence we commenced drawing specie in exchange for drafts. The Mexicans denied this construction of the article, and in consequence, at three o'clock, General Scott gave notice of the termination of the armistice. . . . The Mexicans dare not again invoke the power of our arms, and will yield the point. But it looks bad.

TUESDAY, AUGUST 24. The commissioners have met again to-day, and the articles have been modified to meet General Scott's views.

THURSDAY, AUGUST 26. Yesterday Santa Anna issued a proclamation referring to his great exertions to defend his country, and to the circumstances of the present crisis, and stating his conviction that an honorable peace would promote the best interests of his country. Accordingly to-day commissioners to negotiate a treaty of peace were appointed on his part, who are to meet our commissioner, Mr. [Nicholas B.] Trist, to-morrow. FRIDAY, AUGUST 27. This has been a white day for me. The archbishop's palace is a very good place for the general and his personal staff. It has a splendid view from its top. But since our arrival it has been crowded with the general staff and with a company of dragoons. The courtyard was filled with horses, and the whole place was becoming filthy in the extreme. The chief engineer, Major Smith, and myself occupied a small, dirty room, which we used for a sleeping-room, an eating-room, and an office. Accordingly we determined to seek other quarters. After much inquiry, I fell to-day upon a splendid suite of apartments belonging to a judge in the City of Mexico, which I have secured, and am now occupying with Major Smith. We have a large parlor, dining-room, two large sleeping-rooms, a spacious kitchen, stable, and flower garden. As throughout all Mexico, our apartments extend to the rear, looking upon an open court, with one apartment only on the street. The house is of one story, and each window extends to the floor and opens upon the court. We feel quite comfortable in our new home. The corresponding suite of apartments on the opposite side of the court is occupied by the judge's clerks and law students. We have been much indebted in securing these apartments to the good offices of Mr. Jameson, a Scotch merchant of wealth in the City of Mexico, who resides in Tacubaya. He is our next-door neighbor, and will make a most pleasant acquaintance. Just opposite us, he is now building a most elegant mansion in the midst of a garden laid out in the English style. Last evening Mason and myself took a walk on the top of an eminence in rear of the palace, where we had a most beautiful view of the City of Mexico and its neighboring lakes. We both thought of Newport, and of the thousand delightful recollections that cluster around it. Mason is in fine health, and has greatly distinguished himself in the recent operations. We both hope to see Newport before the close of the year.

SATURDAY, AUGUST 28. To-day I have for once felt entirely recovered from the fatigues of the recent operations in the valley, and have twice mounted my horse, and to-morrow I think of going to the village of Mixcoac, some two and a half miles from this place, where Pillow's division is quartered. Captain Pitman is there with the 9th infantry. The colonel of this regiment, [Trueman B.] Ransom, is a very fine officer. I saw General Pierce to-day. He was not recovered from the effects of a fall from his horse on the battle-ground of the 19th instant, but was able to be about. He was not wounded, as I have before written. He is making a fine impression upon the whole service.

The casualties are much higher than any one anticipated, — over one thousand killed and wounded (about 1060). General Pierce's command suffered to the extent of about 160; General Cadwallader's, about 100; General Shield's, 200; General Worth's 336; General Twiggs's, 260.

CHAPTER 17   They Were
Humbugging Us

Contreras and Churubusco were disastrous for the Mexicans. "The loss of the enemy must be immense," wrote an American officer. "It was a wonderful victory and undoubtedly the greatest battle our country has ever fought, and I hope will bring peace." The Mexicans had, in fact, suffered heavy casualties, but so had the Americans. Scott, who had decided against an immediate assault on the Mexico City defenses, agreed to a short armistice. The collapse of this truce agreement was recounted in a letter to his father from Captain John Sedgwick (1813–1864) of Connecticut, an 1837 graduate of West Point and a seasoned Indian fighter.

CAPTAIN   JOHN   SEDGWICK
Letter to his father in
Correspondence of John Sedgwick, Major-General
New York, DeVinne Press, 1902, pp. 120–125

October 1, 1847
MY DEAR FATHER:

I have just sent a note by the English courier through the kindness of a friend, trusting you will receive it, and, if so, that it may relieve you of any anxiety you may have felt for my safety. Believing that accounts and generally exaggerated news will get to the States of such important actions as have recently been fought near this city, I was very anxious till I sent a word to relieve you. In my last letter, written after the action of August 20th, I gave you as true a narration as possible of such events as fell under my own observation and with my own division (Worth's). The next day our division occupied the small town of Tacubaya, about three miles from the city, in consequence of having received propositions from Santa Anna for suspending hostilities to enable them to make some definite treaty of peace. In this it was supposed that they were sincere, for their army was completely routed, and there was nothing to prevent us from entering into the city that night. But General Scott was induced to hold back by representations that it would wound their pride and drive the Government out if he entered it, and thereby delay any chances there was for peace. Their principal fort commanded the town of Tacubaya, and General Scott insisted that it should be placed in his possession. This was refused, and the reason given was that if Santa Anna lost, his power would be gone, as it was believed to be already on the decline. To this reasoning General Scott gave in, as he did not wish to lose a shadow of a chance to secure peace. Things remained in this way till the 6th of September, when the armistice was broken off and hostilities commenced. In the meantime commissioners had been appointed and were in daily session with Mr. Trist, and everything appeared to be going on smoothly, and we were all rejoicing that we should soon be on our way home. At the same time, reports were in circulation that they were humbugging us; that Santa Anna was using every exertion to organize his army, and was strengthening his works. Yet General Scott could not believe in such duplicity. But on the 6th of September he had such undoubted evidence of it, that he notified Santa Anna that in twenty-four hours (the condition of the armistice) hostilities would commence. So well had Santa Anna taken his measures and estimated the time necessary, that on the 7th he drew out his army and took a strong position between us and the city, his right resting on a strong work called Molino del Rey, and under the fire of the work before mentioned, called Chapultepec; and his left, extending more than three miles, rested on a large hacienda, protected by an impassable ravine. General Scott had been told that this mill was a foundry from which they were daily turning out guns, and was strengthened in this opinion from the circumstances of their occupying it with all their force. He then deemed the destruction of this mill highly important. He did not wish to bring on a general engagement, as he had not determined on which road he should force his way into the city. He intrusted this duty to General Worth, to be supported if necessary by General Pillow with his division of new levies. General Worth's orders were, as I understand, to drive the enemy from the mill, destroy everything, and retire. The attack was commenced by daylight on the morning of the 8th, by the opening of our large guns, and after a few discharges the order was given to charge. It was now pretty well ascertained that a general engagement had to be fought to get possession of the mill; and to retire without it would give them all the moral effect of a victory, and ours that of a defeat. The battle lasted for more than four hours. The enemy, knowing that only one division of our army was engaged, stood better than they ever had before, but were finally obliged to give way. We succeeded in driving them from every position, for we were not satisfied with the mill after the warm blood was up. We captured all their guns, took one thousand prisoners and a great quantity of ammunition. The loss on our side was irreparable; many of our most gallant officers and soldiers fell. I had a very narrow escape: a ball struck me on the shoulder and knocked me down, but did not disable me for a minute. An officer of my regiment, and a classmate, was blown up in the magazine after the fight was over. He had charge of renewing the ammunition, and after taking most of it out he asked permission to blow up the rest, which was granted. He laid the train, but it not going off as soon as he expected, he returned to see the cause, and was blown up with it. After gaining possession of the mill, it was ascertained that there was nothing there of any consequence to the enemy. Some old molds were found that had been formerly used, but the machinery had all been removed to the city. All this time they were pouring a continual fire into us from Chapultepec, but doing little injury, as the fort was much higher than our position. Having accomplished everything, we returned to our position at Tacubaya.

CHAPTER 18

Muzzle to
Muzzle

After the fall of Molino del Rey General Scott held a council of war. He asked his officers which route the army should take into Mexico City. Some officers, including Captain Robert E. Lee of the engineers, favored an approach from the south, but Scott decided to attack from the west, as advised by Lieutenant P. G. T. Beauregard, another young engineer. On September 13, 1847, the Americans stormed Chapultepec palace, captured the Belen and San Cosme Gates, and advanced into the city. Early the next morning the American flag flew over the surrendered Mexican capital.

In his official report, Brevet Major General William Jenkins Worth (1784–1849) described the actions of his division in the capture of Mexico City.

BREVET MAJOR GENERAL
WILLIAM JENKINS WORTH
Official Report of the Action at Chapultepec and the Occupation of the Mexican Capital
Senate Executive Documents, No. 1, 30 Cong.,
1 Sess., Vol. I, pp. 391–395

Sept. 16, 1847

SIR

On the evening of the 12th inst., having the verbal orders of the general-in-chief to designate a storming party, to aid in the assault upon the castle of Chapultepec, a command from my division, with scaling ladders, was organized, consisting of ten officers — Capt. [Samuel] McKenzie, 2d artillery, commanding; and two hundred and sixty men, volunteers, drawn in due proportion from the several corps. At 5 A.M. on the 13th these detachments assembled at the appointed place, and proceeded to their duty.

. . . I had the orders of the general-in-chief to take position with the remainder of my division, and support the operations of Gen. Pillow. This position was taken at the time and place appointed, and that general informed of my preparations, and of my readiness to support him. Lieut. [Raphael] Semmes, (navy) one of my aids-de-camp, whom I despatched with this intelligence, found General Pillow, soon after the assault had commenced, wounded at the foot of the hill. Gen. Pillow desired him to return to me, with a request "to bring up my whole division, and make great haste, or, he feared, I would be too late." The 2d ([Colonel N. S.] Clark[e]'s) brigade was ordered instantly to advance. It did so, passed on, mingled with the advancing forces, and entered, with them, *pell mell* into the assaulted work. At the same instant, the 1st ([Colonel John] Garland's) brigade, the light battalion, under Lieut. Col. C. F. Smith, and Duncan's battery, were put in motion, around the north-eastern base of the hill of Chapultepec, and moved, in operation, upon the San Cosme route and aqueduct. After advancing some 400 yards, we came to a battery which had been assailed by a portion of Magruder's field guns — particularly the section under the gallant Lieut. [Thomas J.] Jackson, who, although he had lost most of his horses, and many of his men, continued chivalrously at his post, combatting with noble courage. A portion of Garland's brigade, which had been previously deployed in the field to the left, now came up with, and defeated the enemy's right; the enemy's left extending in the direction of the Tacubaya aqueduct, on which Quitman's division was *battling* and *advancing*. Pursuing the San Cosme road, we discovered an arched passage through the aqueduct,

and a cross route practicable for artillery, for a considerable
distance, over the meadows, in the direction of the battery, and
left of the enemy's line, which was galling, and endeavoring to
check Quitman's advance. Lieut. Col. Duncan, with a section of
his battery, covered by Lieut. Col Smith's battalion, was turned
off upon this route, and advancing to within 400 yards of the
enemy's line, (which was as far as the nature of the ground
would permit), opened an effective fire — first upon the battery, and then upon the retreating troops, great numbers of
whom were cut down. Having thus aided the advance, and
cleared the front (being favorably situated) of my gallant
friend Quitman, as far as it was in my power, this portion of
my command was withdrawn. The 2d brigade now coming
up, the advance upon the main road was continued. We soon
came up with, and carried a second battery, and afterwards a
third, both of them strong works and enfilading the road. This
brought us to the Campo Santo, or English burying-ground,
near which the road and aqueduct bend to the right. At this
point the general-in-chief came up, with his staff, and instructed me to press on, carry the garita of San Cosme, and, if
possible, penetrate to the Alameda. Shortly after Brigadier
Gen. Cadwallader reported to me, by the order of the general-
in-chief; and, later, between 8 and 9 P.M., Col. Riley, with the
second brigade, 2d division. The former was left in position
at the Campo Santo, to hold that point, and to the left and
rear. The latter, coming up after the firing had ceased, was
halted in rear of the 1st division, and entered the city, with it,
on the morning of the 14th.

Here we came in front of another battery, beyond which,
distant some two hundred and fifty yards, and sustaining it,
was the last defence, or the garita of San Cosme. The approach
to these two defences was in a right line, and the whole space
was literally swept by grape, canister, and shells, from a heavy
gun and howitzer; added to which, severe fires of musketry
were delivered from the tops of the adjacent houses and
churches. It hence became necessary to vary our mode of

operations. Garland's brigade was thrown to the right, within and masked by the aqueduct, and instructed to dislodge the enemy from the buildings in his front, and endeavor to reach and turn the left of the garita, taking advantage of such cover as might offer, to enable him to effect these objects. Clark[e]'s brigade was, at the same time, ordered to take the buildings on the left of the road, and, by the use of bars and picks, burrow through from house to house, and, in like manner, carry the right of the garita. While these orders were being executed, a mountain howitzer was placed on the top of a commanding building on the left, and another on the church of San Cosme on the right, both of which opened with admirable effect. The work of the troops was tedious, and necessarily slow, but was greatly favored by the fire of the howitzers. Finally, at 5 o'clock, both columns had reached their positions, and it then became necessary, at all hazards, to advance a piece of artillery to the evacuated battery of the enemy, intermediate between us and the garita. Lieut. [Henry] Hunt was ordered to execute this duty, which he did in the highest possible style of gallantry; equally sustained by his veteran troops, with the loss of one killed and four wounded, out of nine men, although the piece moved at full speed over a distance of only one hundred and fifty yards; reaching the breastwork, he came muzzle to muzzle with the enemy. It has never been my fortune to witness a more brilliant exhibition of courage and conduct. The moment had now arrived for the final and combined attack upon the last stronghold of the enemy in my quarter; it was made, by our men springing, as if by magic, to the tops of the houses into which they had patiently and quietly made their way with the bar and pick, and to the utter surprise and consternation of the enemy, opening upon him, within easy range, a destructive fire of musketry. A single discharge, in which many of his gunners were killed at their pieces, was sufficient to drive him in confusion from the breastworks; when a prolonged shout from our brave fellows announced that we were in possession of the garita of San Cosme, and already in the city of Mexico.

At this point we again had the pleasure to meet the [Mexican] president [and] general-in-chief, took one of his aids-de-camp, Captain Jose Ma. Castanary, and several superior officers, with many other equally unimportant prisoners; and one of my most gallant and leading subalterns had the gratification of eating his excellency's well-prepared supper.

The remainder of the division was now marched within the city gate, and Capt. [Benjamin] Huger of the ordnance, who had been directed by the general-in-chief to report to me, with heavy guns, some time before, was desired to advance a 24-pounder and a 10-inch mortar, place them in position of the garita, obtain the direction, and open a few shot and shell upon the grand plaza and palace, assumed to be about 1,600 yards distant. This battery opened at 9 o'clock — three shot being fired from the gun, and five from the mortar. They told with admirable effect, as at 1 o'clock at night a commission from the municipality came to my advanced post, with a flag, announcing that immediately after the heavy guns opened, the government and army commenced evacuating the city, and that the commission was deputed to confer with the general-in-chief, to whose head-quarters it was passed under Assistant Adjutant General [William W.] Mackall. At 5 A.M., on the 14th, my troops and heavy guns advanced into the city, and occupied the Alameda, to the point where it fronts the palace, and there halted at 6 o'clock, the general-in-chief having instructed me to take a position and await his further orders. Shortly afterwards a straggling assassin-like fire commenced from the house-tops, which continued, in various parts of the city, through the day, causing us some loss. The first shot, fired at a group of officers at the head of my column, struck down Col. Garland, badly wounded; and later in the day, Lieut. Sydney Smith was shot down, mortally wounded — since dead.

The free use of heavy battering guns upon every building from which fire proceeded, together with musketry from some of our men thrown out as skirmishers, soon quelled these hidden and dastardly enemies. About the time of our entrance into the city, the convicts in the different prisons, to the number of some thirty thousand men, were liberated by order of the flying government, armed and distributed in the most advantageous houses, including the churches, convents, and even the hospitals, for the purpose of exciting, if possible, the entire population of the city to revolt, and effect, by secret and dastardly means, what the whole Mexican army had been unable to accomplish. This was no time for half-way measures; and if many innocent persons suffered incidentally, under the just infliction of punishment we found it necessary to bestow on these miscreants from the jails, the responsibility should rest upon the barbarous and vindictive chief who imposed upon us the necessity.

Officers and men of every corps carried themselves with wonted gallantry and conduct. Be pleased to refer to reports of subordinate commanders. Major [Edwin V.] Sumner, reported to me with his cavalry on the morning of the 13th, was actively on service, and under fire, and was advanced upon the San Cosme road, to be at hand to pursue the enemy. Towards evening, the general-in-chief ordered his command to reoccupy Tacubaya. The commander and his excellent corps rendered every service which the incidents of the day offered to their ready acceptance.

. . . I am most happy to have occasion to submit but a moderate list of casualities, compared with recent reports; two officers killed, ten wounded, and one hundred and twenty-nine rank and file killed, wounded, and missing, of which full returns are forwarded herewith; and also a sketch of the ground, &c, covered by the operations of my command.

All of which is respectfully submitted to the general-in-chief, himself a close observer of the incidents of the day.